True North

A Story of Racism, Resilience, and Resisting System of Denial

SAL NASEEM FRSA LLB

https://www.linkedin.com/in/sal-naseem

Published by Mabel and Stanley Publishing
November 2024

Disclaimer

The content of this book represents the personal experiences and views of the author. While the author has drawn from his first-hand experiences and references materials in the public domain, every effort has been made to respect the privacy of individuals. Where specific events involving individuals are discussed, no personal details or identifying information have been disclosed.

The author has strived for accuracy when portraying issues such as corruption, racism, and misogyny within the Metropolitan Police Service. All references to these topics are based on publicly available information and the author's direct knowledge.

Mabel and Stanley Publishing serves solely as the publisher of this work. We do take responsibility for the views, opinions, or statements made by the author. Mabel and Stanley Publishing maintains a position of impartiality and provides no guarantee regarding the accuracy or completeness of the content presented within.

For my Mum and Dad who made everything possible.
For my amazing kids, Kam, Annie, Saffy, Zaki & Ayesha I love you all very much.
To my wife Sophie, who is my everything.

Without you, none of this would have been possible.

.

CONTENTS

Foreword
By Abimbola Johnson

I first came across Sal in August 2021. I'd started to chair a board that scrutinised a national police plan designed to tackle anti-Black racism. A pretty significant remit. A role that I still hold at the time of writing this foreword. Due to his position as Regional Director for London at the IOPC and as their lead on the discrimination work, Sal also sat on the Programme Board for the Police's Race Action Plan to act as a 'critical friend.'

The term 'critical friend' exposes the competing faces of the role. In real life, a friend who is consistently critical of your progress, no matter how constructive, can eventually feel less like a friend and more like an antagoniser. From the critical friend's perspective, the term carries heaviness. You feel the need to read everything in detail to ensure that you are: developing as informed an insight as possible; highlighting the right areas in a timely manner; working transparently. On top of this, the term 'friend' adds pressure to constantly reframe criticism to ensure that it is solution driven, constructive, evidence based, direct and hard hitting but not personal. To describe the work as 'involved' puts it lightly. To add to that, being a critical 'friend' to the police as a person of colour, (Black in my case, Asian in Sal's) in the wake of generations of racism in policing makes it an even finer balance. Being described as a 'friend' to any such institution can be jarring, adding even more impetus to ensure that your own integrity is not undermined whilst ultimately striving to bring positive outcomes.

Over the subsequent months, I would log into monthly Teams calls. The venue for the Plan's programme board meetings. I'd do 'the headcount.' Looking at my screen and mentally registering the faces of the Black and brown people on the calls, their roles, noting when and how they would contribute, the weight their word carried, whether they were listened to. In 2021, the Programme Board was a predominantly white hierarchical pyramid. The decision-makers and leads, mostly white. The 'colour' was nearer the bottom of the pyramid. They sat amongst those who did the day-to-day work of finding solutions, implementing actions and activity, engaging with the public. The remaining people of colour sat outside of the inner workings of the programme, in roles where they were tasked with critiquing the programme.

A pattern started to emerge in the meetings, the officers and staff completing the day-to-day work on the national plan (often people of colour) would put together decks for the board. Those decks would be presented by their, normally, white senior leaders. Then the critical friends, would ask questions, often about material shared only during the meeting without much opportunity to speak to others in their organisations and truly reflect on what they had seen. It wasn't lost on me that the "critical friends" who would ask the harder hitting questions would be the people of colour, which included myself and Sal. I started to welcome moments in meetings when Sal's Scottish lilt would emanate from my speakers, calmly questioning why decisions had been made in a certain way, who had been consulted, making suggestions for alternative outlooks. We were outnumbered but at least we weren't alone in the room, I wasn't the only person risking being an antagoniser by simply doing my job.

I warmed to Sal quickly, I felt a natural affinity with him. He was an Asian man in a predominantly white organisation tasked with solving issues pertaining to racism that he didn't create. He was the only public-facing person I could identify at the IOPC. An institution that was deeply mistrusted by a lot of Black and other people of colour. Particularly those who could remember its predecessor the IPCC and its string of failures to seriously tackle racism in policing. A concern frequently raised with me is the fact that a lot of IOPC employees were themselves former police officers. Sal stood out: a non-police background, Brown, and willing to speak to the press. By putting his face to discrimination work at the IOPC, I recognise that Sal was taking a huge step. He was assuring people that they could trust *him,* that they could hold *him* accountable, even if they had doubts about the IOPC. He aligned his reputation with his work.

There were two occasions when I can remember this being very important:

The IOPC's publication of Operation Hotton in January 2022. The exposure of the depths of depravity in Charing Cross Station's culture was incredibly important and timely. At that point, the Race Action Plan was in its second year. Police chiefs were arguing about the label of institutional racism, many asserting that few *if any* of their officers were overtly racist, and the label risked being misunderstood as tarnishing all with the same brush. They asserted that the days of people being called the 'n word' were long gone; racism in policing now was about 'unconscious bias' causing unintentional offence. In short, they focussed more on their discomfort about the label of racism than the actual issue of racism itself.

The publication of Operation Hotton was, perversely, refreshing. A moment of validation for those of us who were still having to participate in discussions premised on the idea that we were overstating the extent of racism in policing. By publishing the actual content of the messages, Sal made it extremely difficult for these conversations to be pushed into the theoretical giving tangible specific examples of the horrors people faced. Of course, what followed were some officers, even in the Met, trying to assert that these were issues specific to that police station. Promptly proved wrong in the publication of the Casey Review just over a year later which followed Hotton's lead in publishing unfiltered examples of the true state of prejudice and discrimination in the Met.

Then came the IOPC's National stop and search learning report in April 2022. A report that honestly, I thought was a bit tepid, particularly as it started by reiterating that "stop and search is a legitimate policing tactic" rather than questioning the fundamental power itself. A point I raised with Sal directly at the time. But it was nonetheless important, setting out case studies showing the absurdity of commonplace situations in which the power was misused – for example - using the smell of cannabis as a reason to search someone.

These two reports emphasised how much change one determined person could generate in institutions that aren't just not designed for anti-racism work but are themselves vehicles for racism. The reality is that anti-racism work in policing is very personality driven. That changes can often be traced to motivated individuals who keep the work a personal priority, often to their own detriment.

It was on this basis therefore that when I knew Sal was going to lead on the IOPC's homicide investigation of the shooting of Chris Kaba, I'd felt reassured that someone I trusted was at the helm. So much so that I said as much on public radio and to anyone who asked my opinion of what was happening. But, the reverse of that is that when he parted ways with the IOPC mid-investigation, many of us were left with a feeling of concern.

Sal's story is important and follows a long line of reflective books that show the realities of people of colour carrying the weight of delivery of anti-racism work. It can be easy to become complacent to people asserting they are 'exhausted' by 'doing the work.' We hear it more and more often. But the fact is that it's harder for people of colour to rise to senior leadership positions and when they do, their risk of burnout is much higher. Frequently they carry the weight of being a 'critical friend' to their own organisations, constantly toeing the line of being labelled an antagoniser.

The appetite for anti-racism work is waning. The shadow of George Floyd's murder isn't as crisp as it was in 2020. In July 2024, in the US, Sonya Massey, a 36-year-old Black woman was shot in her home by a white police officer despite posing no threat and being the person who had called the police to help her. The incident was caught on camera, but there has been no global outrage of the scale that we saw with the murder of George Floyd. At home we've had the Casey

Review which found the Met to be institutionally racist, homophobic and misogynistic; the Morgan Report which described the Met as institutionally corrupt; and the Undercover Police Inquiry which is exposing years of potentially unlawful activity undertaken by the Met including spying on the family of Stephen Lawrence.

These are historic, present and future issues and when the initial furore dies down, it's the Sals of this world who are left to drive change in the institutions many so deeply mistrust.

Introduction

For the best part of a decade, I worked at the heart of the UK's police accountability framework, often referred to as the police watchdog. For four and a half of those years, I was the Regional Director for London, and the National Lead on Race Discrimination. I was the first person of colour to have held this role.

My tenure came at some of the darkest times in the Metropolitan Police Service's history. The headlines you've seen regarding the Met between 2019 – 2023 from the murder of Sarah Everhard to the fatal shooting of Chris Kaba I will have been involved in all of those cases, holding the Met to account, in one way or another.

Throughout, I was involved in every major conversation surrounding race and policing, speaking to the issues faced by communities in the national and international media. I didn't pull my punches and dedicated myself to the journey of trying to make systemic change within these change-resistant, mammoth institutions. It was David and Goliath, in real time.

These institutions were effectively systems of denial, systems designed to enforce and socialise the acceptability of this denial. My own organisation being part of this problem.

It was my desire to confront this system that left me at the centre of one of the biggest storms to ever hit the Metropolitan Police Service: Operation Hotton. This was a series of investigations surrounding Charing Cross Police Station that uncovered a toxic culture of racism, misogyny, islamophobia, homophobia, ableism, and antisemitism within the Met. The findings became a global news story, bringing out of the darkness into the disinfectant of sunlight, every 'ism' you can think of. The report, and the content I fought to publish in the public domain, ultimately led to the resignation of the then Met Commissioner, Dame Cressida Dick.

The hill I climbed to get there involved incredibly difficult situations and often, putting my head onto the chopping block, knowing the axe was coming for me.

Why?

Perhaps there was an element of stupidity there. But for me it was necessary to do whatever was in my power to try and change policing and improve the trust and confidence of those without a seat at the table. Black communities, young people, minoritised groups and many women. You only need to read the recent headlines to understand the severity of these challenges, after so many years of systemic denial.

My guiding star was simple.

Change.

It's an overused word but change is the very thing that guided my time in this role, others I've performed, and my life overall. The question I ask myself continually is, now that I have a seat at the table, what am I actually going to do with that position of influence? Am I going to recede into the shadows of conformity? Or will I have the courage to persist and act on the change that is needed? Will I continue to follow my values, my true north? That was, and is, the test I continually pose myself.

Over the past few years, through my work and the people I'm blessed to have met I've ended up telling my story. Consistently, and in the most humbling way possible, I've had amazing feedback that I've learned to sit with. People have told me that they connect with my story and that I should write a book.

And so here I am, doing just that.

No spin. No bollocks. Just the truth.

And with the muscle memory of someone who's been there, behind the curtain.
I won't lie, many of these experiences have been traumatic and painful. The terrain of those systems of denial I've had to cross has been sharp, jagged, and angry, and at times it's felt like all the elements were against me. I've been bloodied along the way and many times it's just been a case of finding my way in the dark and hoping for the best. But you need more than just hope. So, alongside telling my story, I'm also going to share some things that worked for me, and those that didn't.

I've spent a fair bit of time thinking and reflecting in order to write this book in the most authentic way I can. As challenging as it has been, it's also been equally cathartic in distilling my experiences into something tangible and in remembering those loved ones who helped put me on my path today. That process will have been worth every minute if you can take just *one* thing from this book, to help you align yourself to your own true north. To understand your own direction.

And, if you do, please get in touch, or tag me on LinkedIn. I'd love to see how you're getting on in your journey.

After all, we rise by lifting each other.

Sal

www.truenorth-thebook.com

Chapter 1
True North

*If you are neutral in situations of injustice -
you side with the oppressor.*

Archbishop Desmond Tutu

I remember watching the news, and realised my
mouth was open.

I didn't think people actually did that, but there I
was, doing just that.

It was late. I was on my fifth cup of tea, and I
was knackered. It had been an intense week at
work, one in which I had ended up becoming
part of a global news story. Something I hadn't
fully processed. In normal circumstances, I
would be in my customary slouched position on
the corner of the sofa, doggedly vegging out;
instead, I was sitting bolt upright, literally on the
edge of my seat, and irritably shushing my kids
as I watched a statement on Sky News from
Dame Cressida Dick, the Commissioner of the
Metropolitan Police Service:

"Following contact with the Mayor of London today it is quite clear that the Mayor no longer has sufficient confidence in my leadership of the Metropolitan Police Service for me to continue as Commissioner."

"He has left me no choice but to step aside[1]."

"I say this with deep sadness and regret."

She had resigned.

Fucking hell.

This took place on Thursday evening, February 10th, 2022. It felt like a tipping point, an unexpected conclusion to the litany of scandals and tragedies relating to the Met in recent years. Operation Hotton, a piece of work I had been responsible for and been representing in the media in the past week, had been the catalyst for this series of events. For this *particular* moment.

I had to take a few minutes for the news to marinate. Whatever my family were asking me or saying had faded into the background - I was

---

[1] [1] https://www.youtube.com/watch?v=e4xlMo7DlJo

lost in my thoughts. Because, whether I liked it or not, a decision I had made had led to this moment. It was a decision that had been hugely controversial in my organisation, but one I had made in the way that I always did, by following my core values, looking at my role and what was the right thing to do. I followed my true north, and it had led me to that point.

But before I get to that decision, and the gore of Operation Hotton, I wanted to explore and explain what I mean by that notion of true north. It's on the cover of this book and its key to not only my leadership style, but also to who I am as an individual, and how I live my life. So, let me unpack the metaphor.

When using a compass, the north we rely on is 'magnetic north' and actually, it changes. True north doesn't, it's a fixed point on earth[2] that we can always rely on and head towards.

Out of curiosity I looked to see when the phrase "true north" was first used metaphorically. The earliest example I've found is from a book for Christians who question their faith by a pastor

---

[2] https://www.rmg.co.uk/stories/topics/true-north-magnetic-north-whats-difference

who questioned his[3]. In this book Minot Judson Savage says Jesus:

"Is the first great leader of history who, by the power of his personal love, has drawn thousands of men out of and away from their most fascinating passions, and their dearest sins…. He has discovered the secret of the human heart, and so drawn it into magnetic sympathy with his own, that in all its variations and vibrations, it is ever settling nearer and nearer to his true north."

Here, that concept of alignment, power, purpose, mission, all come through in a powerful way, through the lens of religion but in the context of coming closer to your true north. And it is interesting that it's been used in a religious context, because although religion can absolutely be a part of it, equally it also doesn't need to be. Because as individuals, I believe we all need to understand our own personal true north.

- Who are you?
- What are your values/beliefs?

---

[3] Page 117, *Christianity and the Science of Manhood: A Book for Questioners, Minot Judson Savage* (1873)

- What do you stand for?

When I was younger, I couldn't easily have answered these questions. While the answers were semi-formed, they weren't yet equal or whole, and I wasn't able to articulate them. But, as I've grown older, I have spent the time thinking about this, and undertaking the requisite introspection that comes with experience and increased leadership responsibility.

My true north is formed of what I call the three Fs:

- Faith
- Family
- Fight

These are at my core and how I conduct myself, personally, professionally, in every which way. It is indivisible from who I am, and essentially, it's my neural network for conducting myself and the decisions I make. My three Fs allow a perfect alignment for me in the personal and professional, meaning I then conduct myself with the authenticity that this naturally imbues. I'm not saying everyone likes that authenticity, in fact I know that *definitely* not everyone does, but for me, it has allowed me to apply a personal moral framework which has led to some incredible things.

Understanding your own true north will require soul searching in order to answer those three questions honestly. And honesty is the key word here. There is no right or wrong answer, and the things that guide you will be as unique and eclectic as your Netflix watchlist.

So, to wind back, following my true north in this situation left me at the centre of one of the biggest scandals to hit the Metropolitan Police Service in recent history - Operation Hotton. This all took place while I was in post at the Independent Office for Police Conduct, as Regional Director for London and the National Lead for Discrimination.

An easy gig?

That's a hard no, and this book will explain why.

But one that I took on with the passion and vigour of someone who knew they would probably only ever get one crack at a role like this.

Operation Hotton was the culmination of nine independent linked investigations that lifted the lid on the cancerous culture festering behind closed doors at Charing Cross police station. My clear purpose here was to show the public, and other serving officers, what this culture actually looked like.

It looked like this:

Trigger warning: the messages below feature material that is highly distressing and should be read with caution.

Officer 1: *"I fucking need to take my bird out, won't see her until next Saturday. Then I have to work. Promised to take her out the Friday after. Making it up to her from when I backhanded her "*

Officer 2: *"Grab her by the pussy"*

Officer 1: *"You ever slapped your missus?"*

Officer 2: *"It makes them love you more. Seriously since I did that she won't leave me alone. Now I know why these daft cunts are getting murdered by their spastic boyfriends. Knock a bird about and she will love you. Human nature. They are biologically programmed to like that shit."*

In sending an image of a Black man wearing a white shirt, one officer asked:

Officer 1: *"What's good about it I don't get it lol."*

Officer 2*: "Ignore the robber...I like the shirt."*

This was called 'banter'. It took place in a series of WhatsApp groups, some containing as many as 19 police officers, without challenge. Sometimes, communication was more direct.

Male officer to a female officer:

'I would happily rape you'

"If I was single I would actually hate fuck you"

"If I was single I would happily chloroform* you"

Other messages openly mocked non-Christian religions and the Black Lives Matter movement:

"Just walked past the big mosque all the fanatics turn up at to radicalise the young muslims...."

"Opened my balcony door and loads of flies flew into the front room. So I got the fly spray and turned my gaff into Auschwitz."

"PWPEHCLM - People with pre existing heart conditions lives matter. Should of offered him a kit kat and a nice lie down. Murdering cunts."

Many cited racism, homophobia, and glorified domestic violence:

"My dad kidnapped some African children and used them to make dog food."

"Getting a woman into bed is like spreading butter. It can be done with a bit of effort using a credit card, but it's

"Gayyyyyy",
"You fucking gay!"
"Fuck you bender... 😆😆"

The worst part?

The people sending these messages were serving Met officers at the time. Police officers who were meant to serve and protect all of the communities and the rich diversity that London has to offer.

Let us take a minute.

How did you feel reading these messages?

I want you to remember that feeling.

There were many more of these repulsive WhatsApp exchanges set out in our report[4]. But it wasn't just messages. There was an officer openly described as *"a bit of a ladies' man, who would chase and harass women"*, and that *"there was a 'be careful when he's around' kind of atmosphere."*

Recent cases have highlighted just how dangerous men like this can be, even more so when wearing a uniform that we are encouraged to trust implicitly. Here, I should highlight that one of the officers found to have sent offensive

---

[4]

https://www.policeconduct.gov.uk/sites/default/files/Operation%20Hotton%20Learning%20report%20-%20January%202022.pdf messages had been in the same team as Wayne Couzens, the former Met officer who was jailed for life for murdering Sarah Everard in 2021[5].

It was my team who conducted Operation Hotton, and I watched as our investigations peeled back the layers to reveal a toxic culture of racism, misogyny, islamophobia, homophobia, and antisemitism - every "ism" you can imagine. It found serving officers bullying and harassing other serving officers within the *Met[6] - the oldest police force in the world, an institution that had become used to monopolising the headlines, for all the wrong reasons.

Operation Hotton started out very differently to how it finished. Initially, it was about investigating allegations that an officer had sex with a member of the public at Charing Cross police station, which was shocking enough. That is, until officers began to come forward with stories and concerns of their own. Some of these officers were victims. This took the investigation in a totally different direction. To

---

[5] https://www.bbc.co.uk/news/uk-england-surrey-62981675

give some sense of the scale of the issues it's worth highlighting what we actually investigated:

- Bullying, harassment, and sexual harassment of other police officers
- Police officers having sex while on duty
- Concerns a police officer assaulted his partner and demonstrated misogynist behaviour and actions
- Use of steroids by police officers
- Deletion of material relevant to an ongoing criminal investigation
- Failing to challenge inappropriate behaviour
- Officers engaging in discriminatory conversations on WhatsApp

What these WhatsApp exchanges showed was nothing new. All they did was provide the audit trail for conversations that have always happened in parts of the Met, and policing overall, for decades. In the past, these conversations would have happened in the safe spaces of the old police canteens or locker rooms (hence the expression 'canteen/locker-room culture'). Now, the new safe space for this prejudice is in the hateful green echo chambers of WhatsApp groups.

The damning thing here was how comfortable these officers were in expressing this hate. Often in large groups, where they were never challenged. To me this lack of challenge was indicative of the wider problem. Did the other officers agree? Where they part of the problem? Were they inculpated into this toxic culture or were some afraid to stick their head above the parapet to call it out?

There is no 'grey' in this area. The Code of Ethics and Standards of Professional Behaviour[7] makes it very clear what is expected of serving officers. But they are just words on a piece of paper if the culture has become *so* diseased that this behaviour is tolerated, accepted even. And this is exactly what we found in this series of investigations, a diseased culture.

Policing is one of the most challenging, thankless roles that there is. It feels like any examination of policing has to say this, but the reason I'm saying this is not through any form of obligation, but because it's true. The victims in Operation Hotton had to contend with this brutal reality of modern-day policing, alongside constant bullying and harassment from their so-

---

[7] Code of Ethics | College of Policing

called 'peers'. Peers that they had to work alongside and stand beside in the face of danger.

Heroically, they dealt with all of this.
Day after day.
Brushing themselves down.
Starting another shift.
Rinse and repeat.

The findings filled 15 pages[8], all of which made for incredibly difficult, but I'd argue necessary reading. It exposed readers to the reality of this thing we call a 'toxic culture', showing people what it actually looked like. It showed how if you weren't White or male you were fair game. The comments on these WhatsApp groups were indicative of the conduct of these officers, and while by themselves they were disgusting, their behaviour and the fact they acted in accordance with this thinking was even more damaging. 15 recommendations were made using our legal powers to the Metropolitan Police service, focused on changing the culture and adopting a more victim-centric approach when it came to

---

8
https://www.policeconduct.gov.uk/sites/default/files/Operation%20Hotton%20Learning%20report%20-%20January%202022.pdf

investigating the concerns of their own officers. All of which I was relieved to say were accepted.

If reading the report was difficult, putting it together wasn't easy either.

When thinking about how those issues hidden below the surface should be brought into the light, I made a contentious decision. A decision that I was certain was the right thing to do at the time, and still do, but a decision that internally in my organisation was divisive.

You see, when dealing with these sorts of exchanges I'd like to say it was unusual, but it wasn't. I had read so many cases where this had happened that I had become completely desensitised to the ferocity of this prejudice from some serving police officers. A depressing side-effect of my time at the IOPC, but probably a necessary one from a self-preservation perspective. Publicly, and traditionally, we would describe the vilest conduct in a really bland way that gave no indication as to how awful it really was.

"Offensive messages"
"Discriminatory content"

These were two phrases that were commonly used in our press releases to describe these sorts of disgusting exchanges. While factually correct, for me, they didn't do the messages above, or the victims, justice. What do terms like that actually *mean* to members of the public, or to those *other* serving officers?

Nothing.

They mean absolutely nothing.

They allow a vacuum to exist, for those who might never had had the luxury of experiencing any form of hate directed at them to start to excuse this sort of behaviour. *"It's probably just a bit of banter". "They have a tough job to do, they were probably just letting off steam".* You might think that sort of view sounds fanciful, but these are comments that have been made to me privately when I've been trying to explain what this behaviour actually looks like.

I had an incredible team that worked on these investigations for several years, and we were determined to do something different in order to out the issues we had found.

I made the final decision that we were going to publish the WhatsApp exchanges. Yes, they were horrific. But, if we wanted to change the conversation on what a toxic culture actually looked like in policing, and what women and ethnic minority officers had to suffer, people needed to *see* it to understand it. I understood we needed to do something disruptive. People needed to be shocked and needed to feel sickened, and it's at this point I'll ask you to think back to how *you* first felt reading those messages.

It's that feeling.
That's what was needed.

But here was the thing, it wasn't something that had ever been done before. It seems obvious now with hindsight but because it had never been done before and had the potential to be disruptive, I was faced with a real wall of resistance internally. That system of denial, which I'll keep coming back to. Both in terms of publishing the exchanges and even the report.

Why?

The one thing that oppresses better than anything else is fear.

Some of those senior people around me were reluctant to push the envelope any further than was the bare minimum. It led to *many* difficult conversations. There was huge pressure on me to conform and do what we had always done, but those same approaches had never generated the awareness needed on the issues surrounding police culture. I believed publishing the report *and* the WhatsApp messages was absolutely the right thing to do. It was following my statutory mandate in its purest form, unaffected by any other nonsensical thinking.

During a particularly ulcer-inducing meeting, in which I was being blocked off at every turn by a couple of senior individuals, I vividly remember being asked by one of them.

"But what about Cress?"

I took a breath.

This was in reference to the then Met Commissioner Dame Cressida Dick. Years later, I still cannot understand the mentality of that question. To me, it was totally revealing of the motivations of that particular individual and even the use of her nickname gave a lot away. When I heard that remark, I only had one question:

41

"What about her?"

I didn't say this from a place of malice or indifference. I didn't. But I did say it from a place of frustration because what did that thinking have to do with anything?

The Commissioner was *never* part of our investigation and so still to this day, that really sticks in my throat. Never in that particular conversation was there *any* mention of the victims by that individual, and that's who I cared about in this scenario - people who would be carrying that trauma, possibly for the rest of their lives. But instead, the primary concern of someone I worked with was the potential impact my decision might have on the Commissioner.

Ultimately, I was asked to remove the WhatsApp messages from the report, but I refused.

Look, doing what we were doing meant fulfilling our role as a regulator, without fear or favour. Living and breathing our independence, even when that was incredibly difficult. So, any thinking to me which fell outside this mandate sat totally outside of my values. I had no option but to fight for the glimmer of opportunity to make real change, and so, I fought and drew my line in the sand.

When I look back now, I've belatedly, and perhaps a bit naively, realised I was effectively putting my job, maybe even my career on the line. But I wasn't going to buckle. I was convinced it was the right thing to do and was determined to show what we had uncovered. I wasn't there to be liked. I have never cared about that aspect. I was there to do a job. But it was patently clear that this decision was on me, and by inference, all the associated risk.
That was fine by me because I wanted to do the right thing, the right way, and for the right reasons.

For the victims who, in the face of one of Britain's biggest and most influential institutions had shown such amazing courage in coming forward in the first place. For my team, a group of passionate, dedicated people who had spent *years* working on Operation Hotton, putting in so many extra hours reading through material that no one should be exposed to. It was really important to me that I did their work justice. For change, not just in the Met, but in every hidden dark space that allows misogyny, discrimination and hate to fester.

The groupthink* mentality I came across is a challenge that at some point, any change-maker will have to face. Facing it isn't always easy, in fact it can be really difficult. It can leave you draining your reservoir of resilience and questioning your own sanity.

---

*Groupthink:

A phenomenon that occurs when the desire for group consensus overrides people's common-sense desire to present alternatives, critique a position, or express an unpopular opinion.
Here, the desire for group cohesion effectively drives out good decision-making and problem solving.

Nothing about Operation Hotton was personal. It was only ever about accountability and fulfilling my role as a public servant. As always, my team delivered, every page smeared with the grim reality of what we'd uncovered, there to be read in black and white.

On Tuesday 1st February 2022 we pressed the button and published our learning report on Operation Hotton, which included all of the WhatsApp exchanges.

And people took notice.

- The Metropolitan Police issued a public apology, stating that they were *"deeply sorry to Londoners"*.
- Bas Javid, Deputy Assistant Commissioner at the Met said he was *"angry and disappointed at the officers' behaviour, recognising a need for 'real change"*.
- Sadiq Khan, the Mayor of London publicly stated that he was *"utterly disgusted"* by the findings, subsequently launching an intervention in which the then Commissioner, Dame Cressida Dick was put on notice. (*In a meeting that took place in the aftermath of Operation Hotton - he stated in well-documented terms that unless urgent reform happened within the force, he could and would withdraw confidence in her*).
- It was debated on the front benches of Parliament, with Ministers highlighting issues with supervision and leadership within the Met and echoing the need for urgent reform.

But it wasn't just the system which stood up and took notice. Operation Hotton became a global news story.

It was plastered across the front pages, and in hundreds of articles that quickly circulated around the world, from India to America. Requests for TV interviews came in thick and fast - and, although I had a face for radio, it wasn't about my discomfort or personal preference to stay out of the spotlight. I needed to step up. I knew I needed to accept each and every opportunity to talk about the issues, and the victims who remained at the heart of it.

At every opportunity, I wanted to pierce the myth of these cultural issues being confined to just "a few bad apples". The full metaphor is actually one bad apple spoils the barrel. The barrel here being the culture of the Met and to my mind, those bad apples were rotting this culture from the inside, out. And I made sure to say this. There were lots of surreal moments in that period, being interviewed on Good Morning Britain was definitely one of them.

It all looks glamorous, and the interviews looked reasonably polished, but the reality was a bit different. Behind the screen I was sat in my living room as my family hushed into the other room watching me simultaneously on the TV while listening excitedly from across the hallway. I was sat at my dining table; I didn't have the right sort of laptop to do these interviews so had to improvise. I had three shoe boxes balanced on top of each other, and then my mobile phone perched perilously on the very top to get it to the right level. It looked like some sort of crap amateur Jenga. Never mind nerves for the interview, I was just trying desperately to keep my body still so I wouldn't shake the boxes. I had visions of everything toppling with my trainers tumbling out, exposing my half-arsed camera set up. And all this was to a chorus of Susannah Reid offscreen saying repeatedly *"I can't hear him, I can't hear him."*, which wasn't off-putting at all.

I was also featured in Stylist magazine, something I can guarantee had absolutely nothing to do with my fashion sense. In an article that spoke directly to Operation Hotton, leading charities in the Violence against Women and Girls space spoke to the issues highlighted; Refuge, Rape Crisis, and Solace Women's Aid, to name just a few.

Links were made to cases that depicted just how dangerous the issues uncovered truly were, including the horrific murder of Sarah Everard, a 33-year-old woman lured to her death by a police badge, and killed with a police-issue work belt. The article encouraged readers to join a campaign against such disgrace, with #EnoughisEnough and #TooManyBadApples just two of the hashtags that started to trend. One quote that stuck in mind was that of gender equality charity, the Fawcett Society:

"Reading about the messages shared between these officers sends a shiver down your spine. Racism and misogyny are never acceptable but it's even more important that these attitudes are rooted out in the police because this is a group of people with so much power. This has to be addressed. Women, people of colour, those in the LGBTQ+ community deserve and demand better."

The depravity of the officers' remarks meant they had managed to target and offend virtually every section of society. This meant the fury from the media was felt by magazines and outlets that would never traditionally have carried our press releases. The story had transcended our traditional borders, it had become something else.

The public were sickened, and they demanded better.

That in itself validated my decision to publish the report, and the messages. It lifted the lid on what a toxic culture actually looked like, here within the Met. When that lid was opened, the putrid stench of what was inside was overwhelming.

And it wasn't just the public, policing as a whole had to stand up and listen.

Operation Hotton helped change the national conversation on policing culture, providing a template for other discussions to follow. Since then, many have adopted this approach in Hotton, following suit in publishing WhatsApp exchanges or relevant evidence, to show exactly the nature of the misconduct in question. What was considered radical originally, has now become the template. The review conducted by Baroness Casey[9] is just one example following on from Operation Hotton, that has only served to reinforce the need to be bolder, to say it how it is and address the elephants in the room.

Every force, including the Met, had to look at itself in the mirror.

---

[9] https://www.met.police.uk/police-forces/metropolitan-police/areas/about-us/about-the-met/bcr/baroness-casey-review/

What had happened to the Met could happen to any force, and so there was an urgent need for forensic housekeeping. Questions had to be asked about the conduct of officers behind closed doors, and the need for real safe spaces where those subjected to abuse, harassment or inappropriate behaviour could stand up and challenge, without fear of further bullying or, career suicide. It spoke of the need for colleagues to be up-standers and not bystanders to this type of hateful conduct, sending out a message for everyone to hear that there was no longer a hiding place in policing for such bile.

I'm under no illusion whatsoever that, bold as this report was, it alone could never fix the issues uncovered by Operation Hotton, which aren't unique to the Met. These issues are systemic and would fill far more than 15 pages. The issues cited by this report, and many others, have been cited many times before, the Macpherson report is just one that I can point to. Sir William Macpherson spoke to issues of police culture and institutional racism a generation ago. Like Macpherson, taking off the lid and showing a culture for what it *really* looked like was powerful and made an impact. It was once the dust had settled and the lights had stopped flashing that I came to realise just *how* impactful Hotton had been, and that it was a significant moment for policing.

Naively, given the reaction this work received, I expected positive feedback internally, particularly from those that had resisted my decision to publish the messages, and report. I thought they might acknowledge the impact it had made, not for me but the team, for *their* incredible work.

With a couple of notable exceptions, the prevailing view was...

...tumbleweed.

I was ghosted.

My emails were blanked, and I was met with a deafening silence. It was so embarrassingly loud that others around me noticed. I'm rarely lost for words, but I didn't know what to say to my team who had spent years working on these investigations, I was gutted for them.

Personally? I didn't care.

I'd budgeted for that in the price you pay for real, tangible change. If I felt like a pariah in standing alone to do what I felt was the right thing to do I was okay with that, and I still am. The validation

I received was unexpectedly from external sources that I had expected the most resistance from.

Serving officers.

I had so many that contacted me privately, a few who I had met, but most who I hadn't. Some were from the Met, but many were from other police forces across England, Wales and Scotland. A Chief Constable even wrote me a really lovely email. I was expecting push-back and instead, they all thanked me. There were so many messages, but the unifying comment was one of relief. That *finally* someone had brought this toxic culture out into the light.

I was overwhelmed and inundated with messages from people who had taken the time to reach out and thank me for what we had done, sharing their own horrible experiences, some of whom had clearly also suffered. Who had been victims. Individuals who didn't necessarily have a seat at the table but were desperate for change. In the moments I was made to feel like a pariah, those messages kept me going.
So, thank you, to each and every person who reached out.

I can't say thank you without mentioning the officers who were brave enough to speak to us about their experiences. Coming forward took huge courage. The victims who came forward to shed light on what was going on were physically frightened. They openly voiced how, in sharing their concerns, they risked opening the floodgates to more abuse and harassment.

The Metropolitan Police Service is by far the largest police force in the UK with tens of thousands of officers. It is an institution with a yearly budget of over £3 billion that is entrusted in policing nearly 9 million Londoners, even the Royal Family. In essence, by stepping forward they were taking on this beast of an institution, this system of denial.
The officers knew all of this and yet still put their heads above the parapet.

That's what courage looks like.

My mouth was still open.

I obviously couldn't have predicted what would have happened by taking the decision that I did. It had clearly acted as the catalyst for the Mayor of London to get involved and ultimately to that moment when Commissioner Dick resigned. The causal chain to all of that?

Me.

It took me a fair bit of time to digest all of that, and to deal with the inevitable incontinence, and denial that came within some senior quarters of my organisation as a result of what happened with the Commissioner. There were some in the organisation who would much rather the report had never been published than deal with all of this rather inconvenient change which was now happening.

I remember one of my contemporaries even taking the time to "survey" a few of their regional stakeholders, including some Police and Crime Commissioners, to make the case on why we shouldn't have taken the approach that we did in Hotton. I sat watching all of this unfold in the meeting. Fucking furious. Typically, no one challenged them, except me, as was depressingly inevitable. But I challenged their nonsense my way, evidence based, composed, refusing to fall into the trap of ending up as the angry ethnic minority in the corner. I made my point. It became clear to me at the time that there was also a curious motivation to be seen to be putting me 'back in my box'. To fully evidence my point here, you only need to look at the IOPC Impact Report for that year[10]. Despite my representations, to again recognise the team's work, Operation Hotton is mentioned in passing only. The organisational embarrassment was evident, as it was hidden towards the end of the report.

Out of sight, a footnote.

Once I got through this period and had the time to reflect, I just came back to the same thought, all I did here was the right thing.

Nothing more.
Nothing less.

I just followed my true north and made a hard decision for what I believed were the right reasons, and it led to a level of systemic change. A change in the leadership at the Met and a change in the understanding and discussion of the issues around police culture nationally.

This is what can happen.

10

https://www.policeconduct.gov.uk/sites/default/files/documents/IOPC_Impact_Report_2022_0.pdf

This was just one chapter of my life which exemplified when and how change can happen. Now, I wanted to delve a bit deeper into this point on change and the challenges in driving it. Why? Because I am not the first and won't be the last to face adversity in the journey to simply *tell it how it is.*

I have my own reasons for feeling the need to drive and make change in the way that I do, and in picking up this book perhaps you do, too. I'll share those reasons with you throughout this book, in the most honest and human way that I can. Because I wish someone had sat me down all those years ago, looked at me clear-eyed and told me how hard it might be, and how to navigate those difficulties. I've spoken at length with fellow change-makers, all people of colour, who are working hard to clear the path of debris left by others and in one way or another they all say the same thing.

It's exhausting.
And it is.
It is absolutely exhausting.

Fighting the good fight to drive change in systems and structures that are expert and well-established is *exhausting*. The fact that 70%[11] of all organisational change-making efforts fail shows this. If you're not careful, it can take everything from you, leaving you nothing but a husk. Hollow and empty. It's crucial that you stay whole, for your own sake, and in order to drive the change that you want to see. That doesn't mean keeping quiet or knowing when to back down, absolutely not. It means just the opposite.

When I talk about the need to stay whole, I often think of an apple. Yep, an ironic choice of fruit here. Imagine yourself full, red, and ripe, no bruises to speak of with a glossy red sheen. Every time you deviate from the direction your soul tells you to take (your true north), each time you compromise, a chunk is taken away. The first bite won't get you, but chunk by chunk eventually those bites will get to your core, until...
...nothing is left of you.

It may appear the easier option on the face of things, but as I remind myself regularly:

The easy thing to do and the right thing to do are rarely the same thing.

---

[11] https://www.mckinsey.com/featured-insights/leadership/changing-change-management

Small acts of courage can lead to big changes and here, they did. I could have compromised and had a chunk taken, my life in the short-term would have been so much easier.

But, I just couldn't do it.

If you want to drive change you need to retain this moral courage and make the decisions which will still allow you to look at yourself in the mirror, even if they're not popular. Especially when they're not popular. Swimming against this tide will leave you knackered and it's for these very reasons that I wanted to write this book. I don't have any definitive answers, and would never claim to, but I have ended up shaking more than a few apple carts, so I know what it takes to make that journey.

Travelling to and following your true north is a powerful choice, and a life-affirming way to live and work. Every single one of us has the power to make that journey and choice.
In this book I'll show you how I've practiced this, the associated cost and what I've learned on my journey, a journey that has taken me across a landscape where the mountains of racism, resilience and systems of denial have featured prominently.

Chapter 2
A sunny day in Scotland

"Prejudice is a burden that confuses the past, threatens the future, and renders the present inaccessible."

Maya Angelou

What was your first childhood memory?

A recent study[12] of 2,166 people across the UK listed the top ten childhood memories in the UK as:

1. Family holidays, 37%
2. Christmas Day, 37%
3. Visiting grandparents, 35%
4. Going on school trips, 31%
5. Buying sweets from the local shop, 30%
6. Having a pet, 29%
7. Listening to pop music, 27%

---

[12] https://www.comparethemarket.com/life-insurance/content/childhood-memories/

8. A day trip to the beach, 27%
9. Your first boy/girlfriend, 27%
10. Getting a present, you really wanted, 26%

It's a lovely list, isn't it? Evocative of all sorts of nostalgia. I looked closely at the top 10 but couldn't see that being racially abused by four skinheads made it in there. That's my first childhood memory.

It was a sunny day in Scotland, or summer as we called it, we tended to get one good day. Me, Mum and my two wee brothers were walking quite happily down London Road, Kilmarnock, heading towards the town centre. I was six years old; my brothers were four and two. The air was warm and frankly, the street looked better for the blue skies and happy faces. Then, a car driving way too fast approached us from behind. The warm air was quickly filled with the smell of gas fumes and burning rubber. As it got closer, I could hear noises in the distance getting louder and clearer.

It was a mixture of monkey noises and laughter.

The car slowed down to stop beside us. Inside were four White men, all skinheads, snarling with yellowed smiles and bottles of beer clinking between them. They leaned out the car windows and with their fat pinkened faces started to racially abuse us. As the car had stopped, I stood beside my Mum and my brothers stood behind us. I remember looking around us, people were there, but no one willing to help us, no one stepped in.

I stood there silently with Mum just taking it, even as they threw rubbish at us, feeling afraid but not showing any emotion. I could see from Mum's face she was intimidated but she stood silently, she stood firm. So, so did I.

It was the first time I heard the word *'Paki'*. That's what they said, that's what they chanted at us, while throwing rubbish at us from their car, nothing that hurt us well physically at least. The hurt that's caused by this word may have been diluted in recent years, but I can attest to it being a hateful racist weapon that was used to try and injure me throughout my childhood. That lasted for probably less than a minute, but it was mission accomplished for them as they drove off, pissing themselves with laughter.

Mum gathered us up, and we carried on. There was no thought to report it to the police, and it would have been pointless if we had, back then the term 'hate crime' hadn't even been legislated. Those four skinheads probably never thought about it again, but every contact leaves a trace and although that happened over 40 years ago I can remember that day vividly. I recognise it now as racial trauma[13].

Racial Trauma:

Racial trauma, which is also known as race-based traumatic stress, is the set of consequences that occur when a person of colour deals with racism and discrimination. It encapsulates the varied psychological, mental, and emotional harm that is caused by witnessing racism and discrimination and by experiencing it firsthand.

That one sunny day, those 60 seconds, would play a pivotal role in shaping the rest of my life.

That memory also acts as a particularly succinct abridgement of my entire childhood. A brutal landscape littered with racism, hate and violence.

Scotland just wasn't that diverse back in 1980s; which is hard to imagine now given it recently

---

[13] https://www.verywellmind.com/what-is-racial-trauma-5210344

had Humza Yousaf, the first Muslim, South Asian First Minister leading the country. There isn't even any Census data recorded for that period that is broken down by ethnicity to give context. Tellingly, it was only in 1991 that the Census first asked the question about ethnicity, and at that time out of a population of 4.9 million, there were only 42,852[14] South Asians living in Scotland. So, wind back a further 10 years, and you start to get some sense of the lack of diversity in the population.

This was something we were going to find out when we moved to Kilmarnock in 1980. We were the first South Asian family to move into the town. Like many South Asians at that time, my parents opened a shop. Their route to getting there, however, wasn't conventional. My parents had both gone to university and were very well educated. Back then, however, glass ceilings didn't exist, they were concrete.

My Dad had come over from Pakistan in the late 60s with one pound in his pocket but endless dreams and ambition. He came from poverty with the desire to build a better life for his future

---

14

https://en.wikipedia.org/wiki/Demography_of_Scotland#cite_note-16

family. Mum followed him a few years after. They initially settled in Yorkshire, Dad qualified as an electrical engineer and used to build something secret involving tanks for the Government. He actually signed the Official Secrets Act, and never did tell me exactly what it was he built. Time after time, he was overlooked for promotion. His boss on the other hand was more than happy to take the credit for all of his work and in return, blocked any promotion that came his way.

Dad made a really brave decision and quit, without having another job to go to. My parents made the decision to build something for themselves, where they set their own ambitions and removed those ceilings. They were a true tag-team, complimenting and supporting each other beautifully. This is when they decided to move to Scotland and bought the shop.

The shop sat proudly on Hill Street on its own plot. Unusually it had its own car park and was probably the size of a large-ish Tesco Express. Mum and Dad bought it from the original owner, Mr. Hanlon, who built the shop himself in the 1950s. He was retiring and wanted to pass the shop to someone who could build their future with it. He was actually offered more money for it by someone else, but remarkably chose my parents' bid because he could see that the shop would be given the same love, care, and attention that he and his family had over the past 30 years.

I remember the first time we came into the shop it was all mahogany counters and blue and white lino tiles. My Dad encouraged me and my brothers to go behind the counter to where the chocolates were and help ourselves. I looked at him. He nodded and smiled:

"This is yours now."

It was the stuff of dreams, to have your pick of any sweet you fancied.

I still remember the first chocolate I grabbed; it was a Mackintosh's Golden Cup. Wrapped up in pure 70s packaging, golden tinfoil with a white label and shouty yellow lettering. Five pence worth of waxy milk chocolate with a diabetes-inducing caramel ooze inside. It was amazing. Shame they stopped making them in the 80s.

The shop was positioned close to the famous Johnny Walker Whisky factory[15], which sold its brand around the world. It even made it to Hollywood, with Harrison Ford drinking a bottle of Johnnie Walker's Black Label in the original 1982 Blade Runner film, as the unknowing android Decker. Initially, the area was okay, but over the years industrial decline eventually hollowed it out. The decline turned into deep deprivation in parts, as the cancer of drugs and all its associated symptoms spread across the town. We didn't have any extended family or anyone else to support us: it was just us. As the first South Asian family in the town, the environment was hostile.

And being the first had consequences.

I remember early on, our windows getting broken as the local teenagers gathered and we became the blood sport for that evening. Me and my brothers were all tiny, upset and crying. My parents were frantic with worry. I remember hearing the glass cracking and fracturing as the window got pelted with rocks. This was just as I had started school and the message was quite literally loud, and clear, we weren't wanted.

---

[15] https://www.johnniewalker.com/en-gb/whisky-guide/the-johnnie-walker-story/

When we first moved to Kilmarnock we stayed in social housing. It was a colourless, grim, frightening housing scheme called 'The Courts'. It was all concrete and roughcast, a million shades of grey; it looked and felt desolate. We stayed there for a while, and it was hard, the people were hard, attitudes were hard. Life was even harder.

One day Mum took us to visit her new friend in the scheme. They were having tea and chatting, and I was bored out my brain, biscuits piled on a plate in front of me. As I stuffed my face I sat staring out of the window, peering through the tatty net-curtains, when something caught my eye. Pulling myself up to the windowsill, I watched two lads tying another boy to a lamppost, you could tell they were joking about in the beginning. One of the boys walked off and came back into view, dragging behind him one of those old plastic curtain rails you used to get. He stood over the boy strapped to the lamppost, paused, and then suddenly started whipping the boy's head with the long plastic strip.

The other boy watched with his mouth wide open. I watched with my mouth open.

Whack. Whack. Whack.

Blood, everywhere.

After a couple of minutes he stopped, dropped the curtain rail, gesticulating at the half-conscious boy, before walking off. The other boy untied his mate and put his arm round and dragged him away, a speckled trail of blood forming behind them.

My knuckles were white from clasping the windowsill. I eventually let go and sat back down without saying a word. Numb, processing, and waiting for Mum to finish her tea so we could go home.

I didn't finish my biscuits.

The racism was that bad at my primary school, that I used to get confused as to who I was. I got called Paki so often that I started to call myself that.

A Paki.

A poisonous word that many these days don't appreciate the full significance of. One of the best descriptions I've heard of this four-letter word came from Ciaran Thapar[16].

"Two syllables interweaving history with hate, masquerading as abbreviation."

It was only one day when I came home from school and was describing myself in that language that my Mum got upset and explained that wasn't a word I should *ever* use.
But that's what the environment had done, it had made me see myself as *it* did. As something less. Nothing more than an obscenity.

But it wasn't just the kids; sometimes it was the teachers, too.

At primary school, for some reason, we ended up with the same teacher for three years in a row and she was truly horrible. She didn't like me, and at that age I was never sure why. As an adult I now look back and can't help but draw the conclusion that my race must've played a part, because I was just this little malfunctioning nerd who, 99% of the time, was too scared to misbehave. It was evident that generally she didn't like kids, as she spent most of her day

---

[16] https://www.gq-magazine.co.uk/politics/article/britain-racism-paki-word

shouting at us and I'm positive she didn't know half the time *why* she was shouting. If you dislike kids that much, why choose that profession?

When I was about nine years old, probably due to all of the bullying and subsequent trauma, I had a physical tic which had become much more pronounced. Sometimes, I used to tic my head back suddenly. There wasn't much awareness around neurodivergence back then, but I don't think it's unreasonable to expect that a teacher witnessing this type of behaviour might have displayed some semblance of professional or pastoral curiosity into whether or not a child in their class was ok or needed some sort of different support.

Nope, none of that here.

One afternoon she singled me out in front of the whole class about my tic.

Why did I do it? Did I know it was putting off the other children in the class? I really needed to stop doing it now.

No taking me to the corner to have a quiet chat, but instead calling me out on something that I should never have been called out on. Something I had no control over. All in front of a pack of my classmates, some of whom then joined in, some who just laughed and others who took the piss. I look back at that with sadness, not in the present tense but in the past, for that poor wee boy that I was back then. Who had his head down during all that, who never spoke, who took it all, whose tic got worse as a result, and until this book never told anyone about it.

At an early age this gave me my first experience that assigned authority within traditionally trusted structures doesn't automatically equate to decency, integrity, or fairness. There was also the more fundamental point that some people don't have the basic humanity to be in these trusted positions, and yet too often occupy them, causing untold damage.

But at least our neighbours were lovely. I was in the same class as one of the neighbours' sons. One day he had tried to hit me, so I had pushed him into the mud and ran away. For me, that was near enough SAS levels of bravery - I'd clearly reached my limit that day. Normal run of the mill children's squabbles right? So, what I didn't expect to happen was for his dad to collar me the next day. 'Collar me', is actually being excessively kind, he tried to take my head off. He grabbed me, with his big, pink, meaty hands. He was a thick set, balding 40-year-old man. I was seven years old, a mop of big bouffant hair on a spindly wee body, confused about what was happening. While shouting his racist abuse he put me over the bonnet of his yellow Ford Cortina. I remember the thud as my body hit the bonnet and looking up at the sky seeing the clouds and then, spoiling the view, his jaundiced face boiling with rage entered my eye-line. Whatever he was saying I couldn't hear, I'd totally zoned out thanks to fear and adrenaline. I must have been screaming at this point because as I closed my eyes his fist was cocked ready to punch me. Then, my mum, with the heart of a lion, came rushing out.

She saved me. Again.

As the shop started to do well, we managed to get out of the Courts, and moved further down the road. It wasn't great, but it was like Beverly Hills in comparison to what we had been used to. It would have been lovely if that had been the end of it, but the thing was that visceral hate and racism wasn't just confined to one area of the town. It was everywhere.

When I talk about school and growing up, the only warmth I can talk about is the warmth I felt from my Mum and Dad, who were the best parents. I was, and am, blessed. The home environment they built for us was a sanctuary. I still remember how Dad would do a weekly 70-mile round trip so we could pick up our weekly shop of halal meat, the latest Bollywood video releases and, sometimes, the gorgeous treat of fresh samosas which, to me, were worth more than gold. I also remember how on the way back from Eid prayer in Glasgow we always stopped off at the McDonalds Drive-Thru and ordered fillet 'o' fish and fries. To us that was *the* exotic treat, a proper change from our daily diet of Pakistani dishes. We'd stuff our little faces in the back seats as Dad drove us back home, and then stuff our faces again as we ate the feast Mum had spent ages lovingly preparing.

All of the happy memories from my youth relate to family. None of the comforting glow I feel comes from the place I grew up in. Growing up for me was just about surviving. I didn't play outside; I would stay at home and get lost in TV, film, and art. I was a sensitive little kid and wasn't equipped for that sort of environment.

When I revisit my childhood, now it isn't traumatising. I've dealt with all that. But there is definitely a sadness in me. A sadness that I have never shared with my parents. I never shared it with my dad when he was still with us, and I've only just about touched on it with Mum. Thinking hard about it, I suppose I never told them what was going on because I was protecting them in my own way. Mum and Dad were just doing their best for us, and our family, I didn't want them to be upset that I was suffering.

Again, that was a key formative experience because that trait stuck with me. The need to protect those around me from the truth of what I was feeling or sometimes suffering when I was driving the agenda for change in policing. I had to look out for those around me, it didn't matter about me. I felt that responsibility. Not healthy, I know, but it was how I dealt with it. This is why I protected my parents from the truth back then, and also because they were facing the same challenges I was facing.

Actually, that's a lie, my dad in particular, faced so much worse.

Running a shop in a deprived part of the town was never going to be easy, but the hate and resistance he had to deal with was just at another level. He never told us most of what he had to deal with but let's just say he was on equally familiar terms with the word 'Paki'. When we used to come back from school, we'd often go and visit Dad at the shop. I would run my hand across the car discreetly as I walked past it to the entrance of the shop, feeling for any new scratches scarring the metallic surface. I would look to see what new racist graffiti had been added to the exterior. One time I remember someone spray-painted a 15ft red swastika on the side of the shop.

15ft.

We got death threats at the shop when I was a bit older, allegedly from Combat 18[17], a neo-Nazi, far-right group with a history of violence. Outside of terrorist groups, threats and physical intimidation were the norm for my dad One evening as he closed the shop, someone pulled a gun on him. My dad, adopting the advice from Al Pacino* in the Irishman:

17

https://en.wikipedia.org/wiki/Combat_18#:~:text=Combat%2018
Founding,Charlie%20Sargent%20and%20Harold%20Covington.

""You always charge a guy with a gun – with a knife, you run away. So, you charge with a gun, with a knife you run."[18]

My Dad went for the gun. He wrestled it off the little shit that tried to rob his day's takings. Beaten and humiliated he ran off. My Dad called the police, turns out the gun was a replica, but he never knew that at the time.

My dad may have been small in stature, but he was a giant of a man.

But the challenges weren't just from violent criminals, sometimes they came from the police themselves.

There was one police officer who was notorious in the town, for want of a better word for being 'bent'. He was big, bloated, and bearded, and sauntered around the town with a seething, unwarranted arrogance. I used to hear the stories of how he and his mates would chuck the "*scroats*" in the back of their police van and, using batons wrapped in foam, knock the shit out of them. I came back from school one day and we went to the back of the shop to get a few

---

[18] The Irishman, 2019, directed by Martin Scorcese

bits for ourselves. There, sat in the storeroom, was that big fat bastard and his colleague. They were drinking cans of Tennents lager. His mate looked startled. He just looked up at me, smiled and put his finger to his lips to shush me.

He didn't say a word.

I turned back around and ran to Dad. I looked at the apologetic expression on his face, it told me everything I needed to know, and I didn't say anything else.

He was stuck.

In those days, the power imbalance and fear these corrupt officers cultivated is probably hard to understand now. But, when you're alone, and the pressure is applied, you just have to deal with what's in front of you. And that's what Dad did. Thankfully, their visits didn't go on for long, due to what must have been a change in their assigned location.

But from that point on, I was both scared of the police and also felt a simmering resentment and anger toward them. They had made my dad feel helpless, but they were supposed to be the people we called when we were in trouble. So how did that work? There was nowhere for me as a young boy to air, discuss, or process these feelings. It was just that knot that was left in my stomach whenever I saw a police officer walk by me or drive past, and the nervous glance over the shoulder to make sure they had gone. It's a reaction that many people of colour will understand and is one that is still hardwired into me to this day.

Having spent a good chunk of my professional life working in the system designed to hold the police to account for corruption and misconduct, I look back at this behaviour with a professional lens, and it's all the worse for it. It was my first taste of the power imbalance that minoritised communities face in the UK. My first personal experience of police corruption.

Despite all these challenges, what I saw my parents eventually do was to win people over with their character, actions, and kindness. They established themselves as part of the community, and although there was always some residual degree of hostility there was also a much larger degree of acceptance for them. That taught me something about the fact that people can get past their hate, can get past their prejudice if they get the opportunity to know you.

Because people liked my parents it brought down barriers, it disseminated the prejudice. In that area it led to a level of change.

How?

It came down to being decent, doing the right thing, even when no one was looking.

That is something I try to abide by every day.

Within the area, there were also many wonderful, lovely people who were just amazing, many of whom I ended up knowing for a very long time. Here, I have to give a special mention to the community police officers that used to visit Dad in the shop. As scathing as I was about the previous 'officers', these officers were amazing, and it's from them I had my early, counterbalancing experience of *positive* policing. They showed what it looked like to win trust and confidence from the community in a genuine, human, and authentic way. They showed me that not all police officers were to be feared or avoided. Their behaviour helped restore a significant part of my trust in the institution of policing. Their impact on me was more profound than they will probably ever know.

Reflecting now, this had clearly planted a seed in me which I wasn't aware of at that time, but it was something I would draw on much later in life. While it was beautiful to see how Mum and Dad were being accepted and making ties to the community, for me as a young adult me, it was different, and it remained really difficult.

I was this mixed up, scared kid that was a constant target for abuse and I was about to start secondary school. By this point we had moved to Mum and Dad's dream house and stayed in a really nice part of the town. But I ended up going to the roughest school in the town back then, St Joseph's Academy. Founded in 1955, it was a series of grim, grey boxes with bars on the windows and giant playing fields attached to its side. I always thought it looked like Barlinnie Jail[19], the notorious prison outside Glasgow where Scotland's most serious offenders were caged. It felt like a prison too.

It was a Catholic school, and because I had gone to a Catholic primary it was the natural secondary of choice, except I wasn't Catholic. I was Muslim. It was part of my secondary school experience to witness the sectarian divide in the

---

[19] https://en.wikipedia.org/wiki/HM_Prison_Barlinnie

town between the Protestant and Catholic kids
through the lens of a Muslim boy. At lunchtime,
kids would go to each other's schools and fight,
well because that's what these two groups did,
right? So that's what they did.
Where did I fit into that fight? I didn't.

It made the abuse a bit tricky for some, they
would call me a *"Fenian, bastard",* but then
realise that wasn't quite right so they would then
go for *"Ya Fenian, Paki bastard".* One I
remember was really inclusive and properly
personalised the abuse spouting from his pudgy
red face:

*"Ya wee speccy, Fenian, Paki black bastard,
ahm gonnae fuckin kill you".*

Now that's a catch all.

Secondary school was going to be horrible. And
it was. I was the first South Asian kid to ever go
to that school. If I had been built differently it
might have been easier, but I was just this little
nerd, struggling with my own identity, who
enjoyed studying and loved art. My experience
of secondary school was only about survival.

Even in Kilmarnock, our school had a reputation for being rough. This was partly due to the school's generous spirit; it would take on the excluded kids when all other schools closed their doors. When I was in second year (Year 8 English equivalent) one of those kids ended up in my class. He came from Glasgow, 30 miles away. It was really going some, to be that bad that none of the schools from Glasgow would touch you. I knew I needed to keep away from him, so I did - until we ended up in a science class sat close together. As a class we sat in rows, fidgety kids in plastic chairs tucked under graffitied rickety wooden desks. I could feel him staring at me to my left. I did my best to avoid eye contact. But, as I was looking at the teacher trying to take in what they were saying, I happened to glance at him.

While looking at me, he got one of those pointy compass things we all had as part of our pencil cases to draw circles with and, without breaking his stare, stabbed the pointy end into the palm of his hand. He rotated it like he was stubbing out a cigarette. He did this for 30 seconds, smiling at me throughout, half deranged, half mad-eyed. I put my head down, absolutely shitting myself. I made it through that day intact, and within three weeks he managed to get expelled, even from our school. That's some going.

For a while I was treated as blood sport, beaten up by groups of three or four kids for lunchtime kicks, literally. Sometimes I managed to avoid them, but they used to come hunting me. It was a bit like when Andy Dufrense was hunted by the pack in the Shawshank Redemption, but mercifully without the sexual violence. Just constant. Sometimes I ran, but if they caught me, I always fought back. And I never, ever, cried. Telling anyone wasn't an option.

'Grassing' on your classmates was a sure way to make things even worse.

Something had to give. Turned out that something was them.

I knew I had a growth spurt because none of my clothes fitted me, and I felt stronger. One time they were at it with me at lunchtime and the ringleader punched me in the stomach. At this point I knew a good punch from a bad one, I stood straight back up and laughed at him and said: *"Is that the best you got?"* He walked off quickly, and they left me alone after that.

Weirdly, that boy who tormented me grew up to be a Florist. Go figure.

But sometimes you can't fight back.

One lunchtime, as I stood chatting, a lad from the sixth form ran up behind me, putting a knife against my throat. I was only 13. I remember the feeling even now, the cold metal against my skin and the paralysis that flooded my body beneath. I couldn't do anything. I was absolutely powerless, and he knew it. I didn't cry. I didn't say anything. I was frozen to the spot with the blade pressed underneath my Adams apple. I can't remember what he said exactly, but it was menacing. He laughed and ran off. I composed myself, picked up my bag and headed off for lessons. Again, I didn't tell anyone.

I swore after that, and those experiences, I would *never* allow myself to feel like that again. Powerless and at the mercy of someone else. In following a path where I was subsequently aligned firmly to my values, to my true north, this oath I made with myself was one that I always remembered and resolved never to break.

Although, in retrospect these were pretty horrible experiences, these were the kids at school, and I had a sort of resigned acceptance of that reality. This is what they were, and what I had to deal with. But the memory that sticks the most in my mind had nothing to do with the kids, but everything to do with those in charge.

It was all about the culture.

I was in my second year, and we were on a school trip in the Cairngorms, near the Scottish borders for a week. The only reason I went, was to fit in. I hated all the outdoors stuff and here we had to climb a mountain; well, near enough. Before going, my parents were given reassurances I'd be looked after, being as protective as they were. On the first day at breakfast time the staff came round and put the dishes in front of us. It was a roll and sliced sausage. I said to the person who handed it to me that I couldn't eat that because I was Muslim. They looked at me like I had asked them for a tenner, took my plate back and walked off not saying a word. After about 10 minutes they came back and clanked a plate down in front of me and walked off.

On the plate was a roll. I looked inside, there was nothing in it. They didn't even bother to butter it. I looked at it and felt miserable. By this point everyone else had finished, so I sat there by myself in this large old echoey hall eating my dry roll, with a lump in my throat and a lonely pang in my stomach. I couldn't bring myself to finish it. I left the canteen, hungry and wanting to go home.

But I didn't, instead I climbed that fucking mountain.

I'm not wholly sure why it's this memory that upsets me the most from my time at school, maybe because it's what it truly said about inclusion for me. There was a level of callous indifference here. I hadn't even been an afterthought in their thinking. Meaning at a very young age I quickly became attuned to the importance of inclusive cultures – it became an important component of my value set. I never wanted anyone to feel like I did when I was sat alone in that canteen, made to feel less, just because of who they are. It's why I do the work that I do now and why I speak so forcefully about the importance of outing the issues of toxic cultures.

As school was so grim I used art, TV, and films as an escape. I binged on it in a way that I'm glad Netflix wasn't around then. As a child of the

70s/80s, I loved Rocky unapologetically, and still do. Rocky gave so many seminal pop-culture moments that I couldn't even begin to list them. There is a quote from his final solo, and underrated, outing in Rocky Balboa which really resonated with me as it described the way I dealt with everything that I've spoken about in my childhood:

"It's not about how hard you can hit. It's about how hard you can get hit. And keep moving forward."[20]

Cheese? Probably. But Rocky was right.

It's all about that ability to pick yourself back off that canvas and to clamber back to your feet. It's the act of getting back up in the face of those that are trying to break you and then looking them in the eye so that they understand you're not going anywhere. I may have got beat like Balboa, and whilst physically I was no fighter, I had the fight inside me.

You could spit.
You could punch.
You could call me Paki.
You could make me feel like shit.

---

[20] Rocky Balboa, 2006, directed by Sylvester Stallone.

But I would *always* get back up and keep going. That was my act of defiance and it's a quality which I have kept to this day.

I'm Muslim, and the older I get, the more I think these challenges are sent to test you. Whenever a challenge is sent your way, whether that be a blessing or an obstacle, there is a phrase as Muslims we use and consciously say out loud, which is '*Alhamdulillah*'. It translates to *thank God*. And whenever something good happens I remember to say it, and when something bad happens I remind myself to say it - because either way, whatever is sent my way was sent for a reason.

Now don't get me wrong, I'm not saying I'm grateful for all these things I've had to deal with, because I'm not an idiot. But I wouldn't change it. None of it. It gave me a foundation of resilience; it gave me the ability to get beat like Balboa and keep going, it turned me into a stubborn wee shite who refused to give in. All of these experiences were essential in the formation of my values, in calibrating my true north. Standing out when I was younger was incredibly difficult, and it was really hard not fitting in. But now? It's an advantage. I'm used to being an outsider and leveraging that mentality to my advantage professionally.

My experiences may have been difficult, but for me it's how I made that choice to leverage these experiences. It's how I used them to empower me through that trauma, beyond the label of victimhood, and to something more.

I didn't yet know what that *something more* was, but I was going to find out.

Chapter 3

Learning to wear your inner armour

"Be the cactus, a proof of unsubmission, and blossom amidst the fiercest environment."

Abhijit Naskar

They say that the harder you work, the luckier you get - and there is truth in that. People who work hard create more opportunities for themselves.

No one knew that more than my dad.
For 20 odd years, he worked 15-hour days, seven days a week. No holidays, no days off. In doing so, he turned hardship into opportunity. Good luck or hard graft? A combination of the two, perhaps, but I would argue the latter coupled with his faith.

I lost my dad a few years ago. As time passes and new challenges present themselves, I am acutely aware that a lot of my dad is still right here with me. I don't mean that in a wishy-washy flowery sense, quite the opposite. I have his drive, his grit, his refusal to accept less than what I've worked for, and what I deserve. My journey and how I got here, however, might not be what you expect.

After leaving secondary school I managed to get into the University of Glasgow, one of the most prestigious universities in Scotland. I studied Law, but in all honesty can't say I enjoyed the experience very much. From the moment I walked in it became clear that most of the people on the course came from a totally different world to mine, privately educated with only a few speckles of colour in the lecture theatre.

I didn't fit in.

It probably didn't help that my appearance back then left much to be desired, with fashion quite clearly at the bottom of my priorities. I was strong-minded certainly, but on the outside I looked horrific. Long hair swept into curtains, for God knows what reason as I always wore a hat

and *always* kept my head down and away from public gaze. I mean, *I'd* have bullied me....
But none of that was going to stop me from achieving my goal, and I did. In 1997 I made my parents proud and graduated, a huge achievement for me personally and my ticket to a better future, away from all the shite I'd grown so tired of.

At least you'd think so.

When I left University, while others chased a Masters or went travelling to find themselves, for 10 years I worked in a corner shop, my Dad's corner shop.

There. I said it.

For years I've never felt comfortable with talking about where I started, where my working life started, where I was actually *made*. That's why you won't find it on my LinkedIn or on my CV. That's because truthfully, I was embarrassed. My embarrassment was a legacy, a byproduct of what I had to put up with while I was working there. Here I was, a young man with a law degree working in a shop. People sneered, dismissed me, even laughed at me, and assimilated me into those stereotypes of South

Asians. The worst part? That reaction came from
everywhere, including those in the South Asian
community. But shame on me, for letting others'
judgment cloud my own thinking or making me
feel anything other than pride in the choices I
made.

While I was at university, at the weekends or
during the holidays I'd help my Dad in his shop. I
could see the difference it made to him having
that extra pair of hands. As time passed and my
parents grew older, leaving him to hold the fort
alone became increasingly difficult. The reality of
it didn't sit comfortably with me at all.

As university came to an end, I had the option of
pursuing a career in law. I wasn't in love with the
notion admittedly, but as a career it was a solid
one. Long-term, a career in law would afford us
all the financial stability my dad had worked so
hard to attain for all of us. But I wouldn't be in a
position to make their lives comfortable for a
long time, probably the best part of a decade.
What happens in the interim? Is tomorrow ever
promised? Nights became sleepless.

It was a guilt and a worry that gnawed at me,
particularly as I was the eldest son. So, I made a
choice that I was going to put my plans on hold

94

to work with Dad and make his, and Mum's life easier. It wasn't an easy choice, but I didn't air those doubts with my parents. They weren't actually happy with my decision, but they were never going to change my mind. Eventually, they came round to the idea and, with that, my working life began.

It was your run of the mill convenience store. Fairly decent in size, selling snacks, drinks and all the essential items you expect to find at your local shop. It was the only shop on the street and a lifeline for those who used it. We opened at 6am and closed at 9.30pm, except for Sundays where, by the grace of God and retail laws we'd close at 2pm.

When we started out, the area was okay. My days passed by in a flurry of routine. Wake up, collect the newspapers, open up the shop, go to the cash carry. My day would be spent filling the shelves, serving customers, and doing what I could to help the place run smoothly.

Until the area changed. Smack and heroin had flooded that part of the town, sinking the area and those who lived there into the gutter that is drug-addled deprivation. It was rife. Ever seen a builder with a pencil behind their ear? Where I'm from, it'd be a syringe. Bold as brass and no one phased by it. As it plagued the area and those who lived there, it plagued us.

Working in the shop became like serving on tour in a warzone. I hear the melodrama in my own words, but as a metaphor I struggle to think of how else I can describe that part of my life. It was *such* a hostile environment, and I was under fire, all the time. It quickly became apparent that my decision to work in the shop was not just a good one, but absolutely necessary as I fronted up, protecting my dad and his livelihood in the process.

As anyone who runs a shop will tell you, addicts can become the bane of your life. Every week there was something. While high, they'd steal from us, racially abuse us, wreck the joint on a regular basis. I mean, they even tried setting fire to the shop, with me inside it. The next day? No recollection, brand new day as if nothing had happened. It was relentless, and that cycle continued constantly.

I watched good kids, *nice* kids fall into that space, and it was terrible. Kids I'd known since they were wee, who I would try to reason with, who would still try and stab me in a bid to get their next fix. It got to a point where I didn't see them as human beings which, now I'm out of that environment I'm absolutely ashamed to admit.

How I had dehumanised them was brought home to me when a wee boy ran into the shop shouting:

"Mister, Mister - there's a junkie's hangin affa yer roof".

I went outside, the boy pointed up and there dangling was a well-known junkie. In trying to break into the shop through the roof, he had instead managed to impale his leg on one of the stoic, black pointed railings we had to the right-hand side. Both me and the boy watched him for a bit, not saying a word. I then went back inside the shop.

He ran in after me and asked if I was going to phone someone, and I said I'd get to it. He bought his 10 pence mix-up and went on his way. I left that guy hanging on, literally. I didn't phone anyone. When I went out later on, he was gone.

I look at that now, and I'm horrified. I'm half tempted not to write it down, but that's how bad it had become. I'm not making any excuses for my actions, it's difficult for me to look back at this with the lens of the man that I am now. But, back then, I was truly a product of that environment, and I had learned to look the other way, to hate. Today, I recognise these people as addicts, people who themselves would have been suffering, failed by the system, as were their families. Back then? I didn't see them like that. They were a blight on my life and only existed for their next score, doing *anything* to get it, and the shop was always a target number one.

But it wasn't just 'junkies'. The area was rough, with crime and addiction constant bickering companions. People were in and out of prison constantly. One day they were there, the next they weren't. Because it was rough, people would constantly try it on, sizing you up for a fight and seeing how far they could get.

I remember one lad walking in, cocksure as ever and with the air of someone who had just spotted their next payday, and he asked:
"What would you do if I jumped the counter and robbed you?

Instantly I replied: *"Why don't you fucking try it and find out."*

He did nothing.

It wasn't always that easy. Another day a guy came in, and this time actually had a go at my dad. Red in the face, spraying spit and abuse in equal measure. I saw red, as I always did when my dad was involved, and I went for him. I know what people mean when they say they 'blacked out', because that's exactly what I did. That guy then came back to the shop with his Alsatian, to set his dog on me. I went to meet him at the door, my heart pounding. My dad, who always kept his cool and composure, touched my shoulder and simply said to me, 'No', closing the door. Who knows what state I'd have ended up in if he hadn't.

Another guy who was a well-known alcoholic would often come in. When sober, nice as pie, but he would get *really* nasty after a few too many. One day, I'd thrown him out and he threatened to stab me, threatened all sorts actually. Back then, it was water off a duck's back. I'd heard him but carried on, laughing in his face with a *'go on, do your worst pal'*. That Christmas, he had his 'mates' round to his flat for Hogmanay. He'd had a few too many to drink, things out of hand and he stabbed one of them to death. Turned out he wasn't all bark and no bite.

Calling the police back then wasn't an option, at least not an option I ever thought to explore. Being intimidated wasn't an option either. I felt like Mick Carter; the amount of times I told people, *'You're barred'.*

And it changed me.

I started out as this meek, shy wee boy who would stutter if you spoke to him, wilting under public gaze. After 10 years working in the shop? I was an animal; I wasn't that person anymore. I'd physically changed, with regular gym sessions building my stature. I'd mentally changed too, with the environment reshaping my demeanour entirely. Truth be told, I could be horrible. Not on approach necessarily, but if provoked. I was battle-hardened, reacting in ways that I now know defy any degree of common sense. I'd never fight for the sake of it, God no, but try and steal a can of Coke from me? I'm there.

More often than not, racism was the weapon of choice.

Unhappy with the price of the new smaller Mars Bars? Cue the racist abuse. Pissed off that the Chancellor put up the price of your 20 pack of Silk Cut? Cue the racist abuse. Annoyed that your favourite Orange Aero Bars were discontinued? Cue the racist ab…you get the gist.

Of all the times I was racially abused in the shop, one incident sticks in my mind. One old guy was barred from the shop for hurling the usual racist abuse, he must have been in his late 50s. At that time, the shop's number was publicly available and so he decided to give us a ring to let us know exactly what he thought of us. He needed to get it off his chest and, as these were the glorious pre-Twitter days, so an abusive phone call was his personal vehicle of catharsis. As soon as I picked up, I heard a barrage of racist filth. I recognised it was him straight away and I thought, *"Right, let's see how much you've got in you."*

I wasn't angry and didn't retaliate to anything he was saying, instead I listened and added the occasional *"really?"* into the mix to be polite. As I served customers, I would discreetly put him on hold, and he would wait patiently. I'd come back on the phone, and he'd continue. My silent jousting lasted for 20 minutes, and then with almost an undertone of gritted respect he sighed:

"*Gawd, yer awfae thick-skinned son,*" and hung up.

To some degree, my approach helped me navigate a place that had a law of its own. In a world like that, to have any hope of surviving you have to take people as you find them, gaining mutual respect by the necessary means.
One of those people was a well-known drug dealer in the area. One day, an addict came sprinting into the shop and ran straight into the back. I ran straight after him to see what the hell he was doing. There he was, a hollow man, terrified and crying quivering:

"*He's gonnae kill me.*"

I heard the front door of the shop swing open, and sure enough there was the dealer, looking for payment. He looked at me and I pointed to the back, and then watched as this screaming man was dragged from the shop feet first. At the doorway, his fingers had to be prised off the frame as he clung on quite literally, for dear life. But his grip gave way with his fingernails scraping the woodwork on the way out, and the door thudding behind him. It was like something out of a horror film.

Later that day, the dealer returned and apologised profusely for the scene that had taken place in the shop, explaining that he was owed money but that nothing like that would happen again. This was obviously a matter of professional pride for him, and I appreciated the gesture. I never asked him what happened to that terrified guy, and he never told me.

At the time, as awful as it sounds, I didn't care. Today, I do wonder though.

Another day I was driving to the shop when I noticed a car flashing angrily behind me. I ignored him. To this day I don't remember doing anything to this guy, but I soon clocked that he was chasing me. I continued driving to work, paying far more attention to my rear-view mirror than the road. His face grew redder and from the mirror I could see he was shouting and swearing, while flashing and beeping at me simultaneously. I was nearly at the shop and as I pulled into the car park, he pulled in behind me.

Shit.

He got out of the car, and he was enormous. 6 foot 5, a goatee swarming his face and with a big gold hoop swinging from his right ear. He marched toward me with his teeth and fists clenched. I was three feet away from the shop, but rather than run inside to safety, I stood and waited for him, subconsciously wedging my car key between my fingers so it poked through like a ready-made weapon. I was ready, but it turned out I knew him. As he got closer to me, he recognised me, and his demeanour totally changed. His fists unclenched, and I loosened my grip on the car key. He was almost apologetic, and after a few words he laughed, tapped me on the shoulder and off he went. Two old friends catching up.

It was times like this that made me realise, my fight or flight response was broken. I'd developed a complete desensitisation to things that for the average person would cause a not unreasonable amount of fear and/or distress.

I always imagined that the same might be said for those on the front-line, and research by City, University of London in 2019[21] backs that. Their studies show that a rise in violent retail crime can cause shop workers "long-lasting anxiety and post-traumatic stress disorder", types of stress more commonly seen in the armed forces and in blue-light services. Thankfully I never developed any of these associated symptoms, but I absolutely do live with the legacy of this broken response.

This fearlessness has become an intrinsic part of me as a person, personally and professionally. While I never start a fight, I'll never run from one either, no matter how big they are.

I worked there, in the shop, for ten years and despite the grim reading, I am so glad I did. It gave my parents ten years that I could never put a price on. My dad saw his mum in Pakistan for the first time in 30 years, just before she passed away. My parents went to Hajj together, more than once. Most importantly, they got a regular

---

[21]https://assets.ctfassets.net/5ywmq66472jr/22QfMejeWY bimJ9ykX9W9h/0e99f15c0ed24c16ab74d38b42d5129a/It s_not_part_of_the_job_report.pdf

day off and quality time together. Looking back at that now as a father myself, that gives me more comfort than any salary bracket or job title ever will.
It also set me up nicely for what lay ahead.

I was approaching 30.

Anyone who is around that age will know that like any milestone, 30 is an age where you really start questioning where you are in life, and where you want to go. I decided I needed to do more for myself career wise.

I felt that England offered better opportunities and, despite being a big move and a *huge* wrench to leave my parents, it was time.
I didn't have the option to retrain for an English Law degree, because I needed to work to pay the bills. So instead, at 30 years old I had to roll up my sleeves and start at the bottom of the corporate food chain.

From being someone who was essentially self-employed, I had to learn a totally different mentality of what it means to become an employee, with KPIs, dress codes and the minefield that is office politics. Everything I had learned behind the shop counter meant nothing in this new environment and it was a hard adjustment. I was decompressing from a decade of working under physical threat and reacting with a hair trigger temper. Now, I had to learn how to handle a whole new kind of threat, not those armed with needles, knives or their four-legged friends, but this time in the shape of management, fully suited and booted.

One of my first experiences was a job I'd taken in a call centre. It wasn't the stuff of dreams, no, but it paid the bills, and I was ready to get going. I did really well there, and before long was managing a team.

For some reason, my manager just couldn't seem to stand me. For the life of me I couldn't work out why. I was confident in my management style, my team were excelling, and I was someone she could definitely rely on, but she just couldn't stand me.

Quite openly she would be awful towards me, really rude, and looking back, actually quite comically nasty. There was no subtlety whatsoever, it was very obvious bullying right there on the call-centre floor. It occurred to me, happy people don't treat people like that, so I stayed consistent in my own conduct around her. Even when she spoke to me like shit, I was professional and polite in my response, even if all I wanted to say was," *Respectfully, fuck off."*

One evening, I could see she was really low, so I asked if she was okay? It was just the human thing to do, and it turned out her mum hadn't been well. We chatted for a bit, and I just listened. After that? She stopped, no more bullying and a total sea-change in her approach with me, it was literally overnight. I'd killed her apparent loathing of me with a bit of kindness.

It was too late by that point, I might have been being nice, but I didn't have any time for the way I'd been treated, and so I left.

Despite climbing the call centre ladder fairly quickly, I was ambitious and playing catch up. Frankly, I was in a hurry. I had bills to pay and a family to provide for and with every move I made, they were my priority. In 2010, I ended up moving to the Civil Service. The public sector is a whole new kettle of fish with its own set of rules and quirks to adjust to.

It's a big beast, with different departments covering areas that have a direct impact on the daily lives of the general public. Some people are in it for themselves and their career, others are in it to make a difference. Across the board however, I soon realised that there is a civil service mentality, a high level of risk aversion; a love of 'grades' and above all, a hesitation to deliver anything meaningful on time. I spent the next few years doing whatever I could to avoid falling into that trap and quickly progressed as a manager in the rather weird world of regulation.

Within these organisations, I always ended up as the most senior person of colour. This wasn't something that fazed me, probably because of my childhood. I did, however, become more attuned to the challenges posed to me personally, and the tactics I needed to deploy in order to overcome them.

This reared its particularly ugly head in the earlier days of my civil service foray, when I had the double whammy of being sandwiched between a twisted manager and a dysfunctional team. It was a huge learning curve and during a really difficult personal time in 2010 when my youngest son was born, because he was born prematurely. My life was a blur of hospital wards and meetings with nurses and consultants. We spent most of our time in the heat of the neo-natal unit watching this tiny little life housed in this plastic lifeboat, and each day willing and praying for him to get stronger, that bit bigger, and give us that bit more hope.

Each day I would leave the hospital and steel myself for the inevitable shit I would have to deal with at work. I would come into work and deal with this collection of pampered, spoilt human beings who I later learned had managed to get rid of their previous manager, and were now trying to do the same with me. This was only made worse by having a manager who was obsessed with micro-managing every aspect of everything I did, and then started to play my team off me, for reasons to this day I cannot fully comprehend.

Ultimately, they were trying to get rid of me. I wouldn't let them win because my family needed the money, so I fought. While my son fought from his incubator, I fought for my job. Each day I'd come in and never show the bastards how upset I was, I'd kill them with kindness and carry on, outwitting the traps laid by them.

My son was discharged from hospital three months later, he was a wee miracle and is now nearly as tall as me.

By some miracle I survived that place and left on my own terms for a better job. On leaving, one of those people I managed came up to me and apologised for how she had acted, and I remember her saying:

"We were so horrible to you and yet despite everything you were always so nice."

I just smiled, and didn't say anything, she looked down and walked away.

I think my silence was loud enough.

In my next role, I noticed that there was one senior manager of colour, which while not groundbreaking, meant theoretically it was possible for someone like me to hold that position. It was a new organisation and, for the first time, there was this strange new thing circulating in the office atmosphere, hope. Genuine hope, and optimism at the possibilities, and subsequent sense of mission. Bloody hell, this was new, and I readily got giddy on it.

I threw myself *really* hard into this role and within six months had passed probation, performing so well that I secured more than the agreed pay bump. Within another six months I was the top performer for all metrics in the whole organisation, and I was tasked with sharing the recipe of my secret sauce for the benefit of everyone. I think they called it an opportunity.

This early success led to an internal promotion, which at that time for me, was a first. It had nothing to do with building networks, going to the pub with the team, getting the ear of my boss but it *did* have everything to do with me, working like a bastard. My view was, and still is - by being brilliant at your role, you can't be ignored or marginalised - at least not as easily.

My theory was proven when I bumped into one of the recruiting managers:
"You do know if you hadn't been so exceptional in your current role you wouldn't have got the job?"

I smiled and laughed awkwardly, not quite sure what he meant or why he'd said it. He walked off and as he did, what he said began to register. Years later I still regret not being quick enough to respond, with something beginning with F and ending in off. But there it was, proof that I was held to a different standard. I had to be *exceptional* to break that *glass ceiling.

Regardless, I went on to apply that same energy to my new role and again, became the highest performing manager in that organisation. I was driven by the work and my team was top of every metric. So, what was my reward? I was moved back to the call centre. Same pay, but in every other way a definite demotion. When they told me this was going to happen, I was more confused than angry. I said very clearly that if you move me, I will leave.

Two months later that's exactly what I did. Ironically, when I handed in my resignation the Chief Executive tried hard to persuade me to stay, but why would I? This whole episode taught me that even when you break through that glass ceiling, the structure and the culture won't always share your happiness and may actively limit further progression. I hit a concrete ceiling** that I hadn't seen coming and to this day, that decision to move me still doesn't make any sense. What is clear to me is that I was the highest performing manager in that organisation, and I was told that the performance of my team was royally pissing off my peers. That system of

113

denial then kicked in and sidelined me, and I believe my difference was part of that systemic calculation in its decision-making.

The Glass Ceiling

Marilyn Loden came up with this metaphor in 1978, in the context of the challenges faced by women. However, the meaning behind it applies more broadly, covering the organisational barrier that prevents people from marginalised groups or communities from progressing to senior positions. The key difference here is that there *is* a line of sight to that next level.

Rather sadly, this metaphor has become a bit of a cliche but in my view it does articulate in a helpful way what is a legitimate problem. It outlines how organisational cultures, and leadership, can discriminate and gate-keep in order to homogenise their senior structures.
I interpreted the glass ceiling a little differently. Being glass, I saw it (and still see it) as something that can be broken with some tactical, precision hits.

The Concrete Ceiling

This describes the barriers within organisations,

often taking the shape of cultures, attitudes and policies that actively prevent the progression of people from marginalised groups or communities.

Essentially, it is the very barrier which separates *us* from the senior roles that bring better opportunity, more responsibility and higher pay. It is oppression in practice, and it is a bastard. The term was originally coined in 2016 by Jasmine Babers, to describe the additional hardship faced by women of colour in the workplace, versus White women. The use of concrete is deliberate in this analogy, because you can't break through it, and you can't see anything that sits below it. Without this clear line of sight, senior roles remain out of view, out of mind and ultimately, out of reach for those stuck below that ceiling.

Any credible organisation will have its policies on equity, diversity and inclusion in place that looks to combat this age-old issue. However, the consistent lack of representation at senior levels, no matter the workplace, is a reminder of just how far the UK still has to go.

Research led by Green Park in 2021[22] showed that out of the 1099 most powerful roles in the country, only 52 are filled by non-White individuals. This equates to 4.7% of the total number, compared to the 18% proportion of the UK population. This is something I saw in practice in policing, with no ethnic minority Chief Constables and just one Police and Crime Commissioner. But policing is far from the only sector blighted by this inequality.

22

https://www.peoplemanagement.co.uk/article/1743111/only-11-top-roles-ftse-100-held-ethnic-minority-leaders-research-finds

Green Park Research 2021

How many of the top positions are filled by non-White individuals:

- *No Permanent Secretaries on the Civil Service Board;*
- *No Supreme Court Judges;*
- *No CEOs at the 15 national sports governing bodies*
- *Only one out of 31 Trade Union leaders*
- *Only 5 out of 50 Vice-Chancellors at the top 50 universities.*
- *No CEOS from the top 50 NHS Trusts.*
- *Only 2 ethnic minority FTSE100 CEOs,*
- *Only 1 Advertising Agency CEO,*
- *No CEOs of the top UK financial institutions.*
- *Only 6 CEOs or Managing Partners at the UK's top 61 law, accountancy, and consultancy firms.*

This is the scale of the issue, but that wasn't going to stop me trying.

All I wanted to do was work, and progress, in order to build a better quality of life for me and my family. But, as with every other area of my life, I've always had to fight, for my job, for my livelihood, and for the life that my family deserves.

My fight in these workplaces was with these wee tyrants, masquerading as managers.

In terms of the managers I had, because I was such a late bloomer I had no point of reference so had just assumed it was normal to be managed by a succession of idiots and bullies. I honestly thought that varying degrees of those qualities came with management in those environments. Yes, I started off pretty junior as I've said before, but in my climb, I certainly noticed a few common characteristics:

- Huge levels of narcissism
- Precious egos
- Insecurity
- Desire to micromanage
- Bullying with a degree of relish
- A determination to keep me down.

Even that term manager is revealing, because to me you *manage things*, but you *lead people*. Clearly, in these scenarios I was just a thing, and these were no leaders.

I knew I was being treated differently from peers, but I had never understood why. I hadn't yet understood how that latent racism could manifest itself.

My experience of racism to that point had always hit me straight in the face, more often than not quite literally. It was always violent, obvious, and ugly. Oddly, that was easier to deal with. Now I had to deal with racism in a way that wasn't obvious, but hid behind the faces of smiling assassins, and I struggled.

At my most junior grade, I was among a mosaic of ethnic diversity. The stark reality of that was totally lost on me until I climbed the ladder and began to progress into higher, managerial roles. Now, I know this to be the typical teardrop shape of ethnic representation within organisations. Ethnic minorities are always disproportionately represented at the most junior grades at the bottom of the teardrop, as the seniority increases up the tear, the Whiter that organisation becomes. To put that into perspective, research conducted by Green Park of 100 FTSE firms shows that it would take more than 200 years for the leadership of the UK's largest firms to match the diversity of the working population.

That is how acute the lack of ethnic diversity at senior levels is.

Nowadays, this is pretty common knowledge, with reams of research that acknowledge the wider issue. Back then, it simply wasn't there and was a lesson I learned entirely from experience. As a fledgling manager, I soon realised I was going to be the only one in the room that looked like me. That brought along challenges I wasn't expecting; the disproportionate criticism; the unilateral changing of shifts to affect my known childcare arrangements; the tactics used to marginalise me from influence; the denial of training and the bullying.

At this point it's probably helpful to share the four dimensions of racism:
1. Internalised
2. Interpersonal
3. Institutional
4. Structural

This excellent graphic by the Slow Factory Foundation is one of the best representations of this:

At times I was tempted to drill holes right through that God forsaken concrete ceiling, but I soon realised, I didn't have the right equipment and would end up getting nothing more out of it than debris in my eyes. Ultimately, I would suffer. I refused to waste my emotional energy in trying to dismantle something I had neither the power nor tools to do so. Why? A different ceiling altogether, the *class* ceiling.

My way of dealing with it was to find another role where I thought things might be different and leave.

I've lost count of the managers who would air their *disappointment* that I was leaving, but, I never felt apologetic about it, and I still don't. Instead, I always politely noted their disappointment and then proceeded to negotiate my notice period down as much as I could do, which always went down like a cup of cold sick and brought me a childish level of internal delight.

The Class Ceiling

The third and final ceiling, and it's the socioeconomic barrier that prevents the average man/woman on the street from enjoying the luxurious trappings enjoyed by the elite. Class origin being the key here.

Research from the London School of Economics, conducted by Sam Friedman and Daniel Laurison[23], helped to define this concept. Their work articulated what people living in this country have known for a long time - class matters. They showed that professionals whose parents were employed in working-class jobs earn on average £6,200 a year less than their colleagues whose parents worked in higher professional/managerial positions. Women face a 'double disadvantage' in comparison to men, and for older generations - the size of the pay gap is even larger.

The civil service demonstrates this point quite starkly. Only 18% of senior civil servants are from working-class or low socio-economic backgrounds - while for more junior grades the figure is 43%. The composition of the Senior Civil Service has barely changed since 1967, the last time this data was collected according to a

---

[23] https://blogs.lse.ac.uk/politicsandpolicy/introducing-the-class-ceiling/

Social Mobility Commission report[24].

I encountered this class ceiling when I moved to one civil service organisation as a middle grade manager.

The old military officers club is a useful metaphor here. This harks back to the old military school of thought which had bespoke quarters for high-ranking military officers and excluded lower grade personnel. It was for a certain class of individual with very specific requirements which, if you didn't meet, you absolutely weren't welcome. It turns out that this club is a very real thing in Britain. I just had never been behind the closed door to notice it before. In this organisation, it was a blindingly white peak at the top, which in itself set off the warning klaxon. I also noticed that within the senior structure, the vast majority were privately educated, and most had attended Oxford or Cambridge.

It was an incredibly elitist environment; an inclusive culture was an anathema here. The exclusion of course was never blatant, it never is

---

[24]https://assets.publishing.service.gov.uk/government/uploads/system/uploads/attachment_data/file/987600/SMC-NavigatingtheLabyrinth.pdf

but it was the ultimate system response of 'if you're not one of us you're not coming in'.

I don't sound particularly working class. I actually have a very distinguishable Scottish accent that I haven't lost, and that I'm pretty sure takes people by surprise when I first get talking. But I carry my working-class background proudly, and in the Civil Service I'm not sure this did me any favours.

The higher I climbed, the more my meetings, the behaviours around me, and interactions with me became condescending, belittling and permeated with palpable arrogance. I found it infuriating. It was insidious how this culture made you question yourself. I recall one meeting where two very senior people decided not to attend what was going to be a difficult meeting, leaving me to deal with seven angry external civil servants, alone. It was brutal, and incredibly unprofessional but there was never an apology, or even an explanation as to why they had decided not to attend. Just an air of unapologetic diffidence when I next saw them.

I'd got within touching distance of the top table and saw firsthand what it looked like. It was abundantly clear to me that it would be really hard to get my feet anywhere close, let alone under it. I did my best, until I concluded that my ability had nothing to do with my progress. Once that was settled, I did what I'd advise anyone else to do in that situation, I picked my moment and left.

So, three structural barriers which actively gate-keep and for me personally, discriminated against me in my career. The three biggest tools I needed to navigate through these challenges were:

1. Resilience
2. Resilience
3. Resilience

In each organisation, I worked hard to develop and grow. Once it became apparent that progression simply was not possible, I'd vote with my feet and leave. At the level I'd managed to get to, fighting the institutional racism that was permeated so deeply into these ceilings was a pointless exercise which would have sapped precious energy which I could put to use elsewhere. It's easy to say that now when I look back objectively, but at the time it wasn't always as simple. Each rejection, snide comment, every exclusionary act had the power to chip away at you. But only if you let it. I decided to let those additional barriers build my resilience, every instance fortifying my inner armour, equipping me for future challenge.

I say 'decided' quite deliberately.

When facing structural racism/discrimination, we all have a choice. Do I allow it to embitter me, or do I leverage these experiences to work to my benefit? I consciously chose the latter. My lived experience became my artillery in the fight for my progression, the end goal being a fair crack at the opportunities others took for granted. I shouldn't have been put in the position to even need to make that choice, but, as anyone from a minority background or community can attest to, when you're navigating a system that consistently gives racist and discriminatory responses, we can't afford *not* to.

My resilience couldn't and didn't just exist in my own strength. It was rooted in my love for my family and my faith, both of which are incredibly precious to me. On the toughest days they provided a clear line of sight as to what I needed to do and, more importantly, *why*.

This is why it's so crucial that you find your own true north, whatever that may be.

As a result of my career to date, and I include my years at Dad's shop, I'm left with an inner armour which looks medieval. No bastard's getting through it. It's been forged in two very different worlds where danger and violence look totally different. My experiences taught me how to cope with that, a byproduct of a totally dysfunctional fight or flight response.
But I wouldn't change any of it.

These experiences provided an essential grounding and preparation for what would become my biggest professional challenge, the world of police misconduct, where I was going to need that armour.

Chapter 4

The bollocks of imposter syndrome

"No one can make you feel inferior without your consent."

Eleanor Roosevelt.

"How are you managing your imposter syndrome?"
"It must be tough; bet you feel like a bit of an imposter?"
"You are doing so well! That imposter syndrome doesn't show at all!"
"Would you like some training on 'how to manage your imposter syndrome'?"

For God's sake.

One month into my most senior role to date and these questions were being fired at me from every angle in scatter-gun fashion, despite having secured an internal promotion to one of

131

the most senior roles in the organisation. My imposter syndrome? I had no idea what they were on about. I don't doubt that *some* of these people meant well, but I had never felt so patronised.

In 2019 I was appointed as the Interim Regional Director for London at the Independent Office for Police Conduct (IOPC), it was the most senior role I'd ever undertaken and a huge milestone for me personally, as well as professionally.

I remember getting the news one chilly March morning. I was on my drive getting ready to go to work and the phone rang. I was driving so I took the call in the car, on the hands free.

As I heard the words *"congratulations, you have got the role…..",* I felt numb. Alhamdulillah. I couldn't believe it. I got out the car and started to jump about on my driveway, like an absolute dick. I remember one of my neighbours watching me from a distance, stood at their doorstep clutching their milk bottle and scratching their head as their blue dressing gown flapped about. I waved apologetically as I caught myself, phoning my wife straight away. All I could say? *"I made it."*

After all of those years of grind and battles I had finally caught up in the imaginary race I was running. At 43 I now felt I was finally in the position I should have been. I'd reached the finishing line, way behind my peers in my race time but I had reached the same place all the same. Now I could provide my family with the financial security they deserved and had a position where finally I believed I could make a difference.

To my mind at that moment, I had made it, or so I thought.

I hadn't, but just didn't realise it then.

I had joined the Independent Police Complaints Commission (IPCC), the IOPC's predecessor, back in 2015. I remember reading the job advert for a Senior Assessment Manager at the IPCC, it was a slight demotion from my then current role in stature and salary, but I really wanted to work for the IPCC, its purpose really spoke to me.

Turns out there was this whole system in place designed to deal with police complaints and misconduct.

The IPCC[25]

Formally founded in 2003, it replaced the Police Complaints Authority and was funded by the Home Office. The IPCC operated under statutory powers and duties defined in the Police Reform Act 2002[26]. The IPCC existed to increase public confidence in the police complaints system in England and Wales. It investigated serious complaints and allegations of misconduct against the police and handled appeals. It was independent of pressure groups, political parties and, in principle, of government.

For me, it's the genesis of the IPCC that really resonated.

It was created as a result of a recommendation from the Stephen Lawrence Inquiry in 1999 which called for the establishment of *"an independent* body". In April 2020 the human rights organisation Liberty published a study

---

25

https://www.gov.uk/government/organisations/independent-police-complaint-commission
[26] https://www.legislation.gov.uk/ukpga/2002/30/content

called "*An Independent Police Complaints Commission*", the Police Reform Act 2002 created the IPCC the following year. So, for the first time in the history of policing in England and Wales there was an independent body in place which had the power to conduct independent investigations into the police service.

This was a real milestone, because the two predecessors to the IPCC suffered because of their lack of power.

The first independent body to hold the police to account was set up in 1977 following the corruption scandals in the Metropolitan Police Service. This was named the Police Complaints Board. In practice it was impotent as it had limited powers to act on and no power to independently investigate. In 1985, following on from the Brixton Riots of 1981, Lord Scarman's report *into* the riots led to the establishment of the Police Complaints Authority. While the Authority had more powers than the Board, it still didn't have the power to independently investigate the police, it still relied on police investigators.

So, here was the opportunity to work for a body that was created truly to make a difference. Its roots lay in another tragic seminal moment in Britain's checkered racial history with the brutal murder of an innocent young Black man, Stephen Lawrence. Yet again, the Met were the force at the heart of this national scandal. That was the history of the organisation, and I really wanted to work for them.

My first four years in the organisation were eye-opening. My normal process kicked in of getting up to speed as quickly as possible with the demands of any new role in a way that I became technically proficient in the key legislative framework and all of the legal nuances needed to deal with the various challenges. I also got attuned to the culture, which was very 'policey'. There were a lot of retired police officers who had come to work for the IPCC, and with them they imported this peculiar grievance culture. A culture of management by misconduct. Instead of dealing with the issues and challenges which naturally might arise when you have line-management responsibilities, the first instinct was to treat everything as a disciplinary matter.

An example?

I had a pedestal under my desk, and being the absent-minded fool that I was, in my notebook I kept the log-in details for my laptop, one less password to retain in the brain. One night I forgot to lock the drawer, the next day I was hauled into my manager's officer to say the security team had done a security check (at their request) and discovered my password. I pointed out it was *inside* my notebook, *inside* my drawer which meant they opened my drawer, and searched through my things, looked *inside* my notebook, and then found this password, *inside*. But that detail didn't matter to my then manager. This manager then put me through an internal disciplinary process. I fought this nonsense but unsuccessfully. The whole system as it was then, was set up to enforce this sort of unfairness, which was a theme I'd come back to. This was the culture I was working in.

In retrospect there were also comical moments during that time, that others appreciated more than me. This happened in another role in which I had ended up becoming the elder statesman of the department, which was full of youngsters. Rather appallingly I was known by many as their '*Work Dad*'. Eugh. I had ended up in this informal role as a result of the surreal toxic reign of the Head of the Department at that time. It was an open secret what was going on at that time and we had all sorts of surreal experiences, from a colleague having a panic attack on the office floor requiring an ambulance to attend, to them confiscating a youngster's mobile to go through their texts, such was the extent of their paranoia.

My manager at the time had a laugh that was a louder and throatier version of the comic Alan Carr's laugh. Please just Google it, and you can then appreciate better what I'm going to tell you next.

Every time they laughed, *that laugh* went through my soul.

It clattered about so noisily that I couldn't think or hear anything else. I literally had to stop what I was doing. I took my hands away from the keyboard, closed my eyes until it passed, almost wincing in pain as what seemed like 15 minutes but was probably 15 seconds crawled past. I actually held my breath until it stopped, clearly that laugh was triggering a physical response. What I hadn't realised at that time, was everyone in that wide open office space used to watch this play out, every day, and they'd find it hilarious.

As soon as *they* laughed, all eyes were on *me*, and my barely contained fury.

It was in this role that I gained early exposure to the range of issues police forces deal with through the thousands of referrals I dealt with on conduct and complaint matters which, legally they had to send to us. Anything from the sometimes banal (police officers forgetting a crate of their tun grenades at the scene of a crime), to the darkest depths of depravity. It gave me a hint of what was to come.

Within a couple of years, I'd hit my 40th birthday, said bye to some lovely colleagues, done my first stand up-gig (yes, really!), and secured a promotion as the Head of that department. In that period the IPCC ceased to exist, and in 2018 we morphed into its successor, the Independent Office for Police Conduct.

This was essentially a rebrand, with tweaked powers, new corporate hues of ochre and dolphin grey replacing the turquoise and steel grey of before. Importantly, there was new leadership who were keen to be seen to make a break from past failures.

An opportunity for a six-month interim position as Director for London came up at the end of 2018. By that point I was getting itchy feet and although I was a rank outsider, I went for the job.

In the interview I articulated how I would do that job in a way that was true to my values and aligned with the organisational values. I needed to leave that interview telling the panel not what they *wanted* to hear but what they *needed* to hear. I believed the job needed to be performed in a way that made a difference and spoke to the issues which were fundamentally affecting community confidence, those same communities who had been saying the same things for decades.

Black communities.

This takes me back to jumping about like a dick on my drive and the subsequent low-level assault of people's perceptions on my Imposter Syndrome. Before I get into my own experience, I want to be unequivocal on my position on this. I think it is absolute bollocks.

Imposter Sydrome can be described as the persistent inability to believe that your success is deserved or has been legitimately achieved as a result of your own efforts or skills.

So here is my starting issue. I didn't in any way, shape or form, feel that my success had not been achieved as a result of my own effort and skill. I had followed my true north, with the support of my family, belief in my faith and fought for every opportunity. So how could I possibly feel that my success wasn't down to my own efforts, and therefore not legitimate?

That ladder I had to climb was old, broken, its rungs not evenly placed. It wasn't balanced safely against those corporate structures making that ascent sometimes dangerous. The climb was tough. It was my own navigation of that rickety structure and sheer unrelenting persistence that had allowed me to ascend to the 'top' of that ladder.

By the time I got to the top I was exhausted. There was a huge sense of gratitude to my family and my faith, but *never* did I feel like an imposter. Not because I'm some vainglorious, egotistical arsehole but because I had earned my place there. It had taken so much for me to have reached that level that any attempted placement of the word imposter just rebounded. It's worth tracing back to the origins of Imposter Syndrome. Psychologists Pauline Clance and Dr. Suzanne Imes coined the term "impostor syndrome" when they published "The Impostor Phenomenon in High Achieving Women:

Dynamics and Therapeutic Intervention" in 1978"[27].

Their view was that despite their own outstanding accomplishments *"women who experience the imposter phenomenon persist in believing that they are really not bright and have fooled anyone who thinks otherwise"*.

This concept really caught fire. The essence of this message was extrapolated beyond the original audience to anyone that had these 'feelings' and led to the creation of a huge industry worth tens of millions. Just Google it and see how much is available.

The pervasiveness of what has now become an ideology can be seen in the statistics. One survey[28] of 2,000 tech professionals in India, UK and USA showed that 56% of men and women were suffering equally from imposter syndrome. 33% said they had sought professional help in

---

[27]

https://www.paulineroseclance.com/pdf/ip_high_achieving_women.pdf

[28] https://hbr.org/2021/02/stop-telling-women-they-have-imposter-syndrome

managing these feelings. KMPMG[29] found 75% of executive female leaders suffered from Imposter Syndrome. It is now recognised as one of the most common mental health issues in today's workplace[30].

Just let that last point sink in.

An industry with products designed and prescribed to 'help' individuals, to help you, battle this syndrome that you've been told you were suffering from. But here's the thing, to my mind it's a misdiagnosis.

The original study by Clance and Imes was done in the context of 150 women who were White. That study took no account of how the issue of race and racism intersects. It took no account of class, of sexuality, of the concept of bias. It also took no account of environmental factors. I.e. was the organisational environment that these newly promoted people had entered truly inclusive and accommodating? Was that organisational culture calibrated correctly to

---

[29] https://info.kpmg.us/news-perspectives/people-culture/kpmg-study-finds-most-female-executives-experience-imposter-syndrome.html
[30] https://uk.indeed.com/lead/working-on-wellbeing-2022-report

allow people from minority backgrounds to feel like they belonged in what was very often an alien landscape, and then the alien?

Fundamentally I believe this is what makes the concept of Imposter Syndrome so flawed and damaging. Essentially it says *you* have a problem.

You don't.
They do.
But *you* suffer.

What Imposter Syndrome does in effect is gaslight the legitimate experience of so many people who come from minoritised backgrounds and enter these structures where the environments are pale, male, and stale.

It makes them question themselves instead of appreciating that it's the organisational environment, the behaviour of the senior managers, the culture that they have cultivated which makes them feel that particular way.

It is in essence another system of denial which serves to deny, oppress, and fleece marginalised people in a systematic way. This oppressive system serves to disempower remarkable individuals who have been successful, people who need to realise, but are failing to understand, their own power.

It's an insidious and toxic concept, which I have no moral or intellectual truck with.
This was something I personally experienced once I became a Director at the IOPC. I've mentioned the comments at the start of this chapter that were made to me and never resonated. However, here I was in London, the most senior person of colour in the office, the only South Asian and the only Muslim at that level. In no way did I feel any sense of belonging. The culture wasn't inclusive. Generally, I found this came about because of thoughtlessness.

Then in writing this book I was reminded of this famous quote by Sir William MacPherson and his definition of institutional racism and how thoughtlessness in this context can have greater meaning:

'The collective failure of an organisation to provide an appropriate and professional service to people because of their colour, culture or ethnic origin. It can be seen or detected in processes, attitudes and behaviour which

*amount to discrimination through unwitting prejudice, ignorance, **thoughtlessness** and racial stereotyping.'*
Senior managers performatively embraced notions that they were champions of diversity, but not mine apparently. But I was used to this."

Meetings at this level were all kinds of fascinating. In theory I now had a seat at the table but when I sat at that table, my chair wasn't the same as everyone else's, different enough for it to be uncomfortable. There was an art to these meetings, there was a whole secret language of subtle cues and nuances that you needed to have read up on to take part effectively in those conversations.

The in-jokes at the beginning, the intonation of language, the looks across the room, the slippery shoulderness of it all. It was fascinating and in retrospect it really brought to mind the Art of War.

Shame I hadn't read it back then.

A couple of months in, one of my peers tried to kneecap me in a meeting, accusing me of massaging my performance figures. I couldn't believe what I was hearing. It was a flat out lie. I had worked with my team to improve our performance and we were flying. This other team, however, were in the red and, rather than address her own issues this colleague felt entitled enough to attack me. I wasn't having it and asked her to show me the evidence to support her claims, she grumbled under her breath that she would get back to me later. She never did.

Another more subtle example of this was the leadership WhatsApp Group. No, it wasn't one of *those* groups. It was something the senior team had set up to keep in touch and I was invited to join. So, I did. It showed me a world where I didn't belong. I had made a huge jump to a director role, but I wasn't minted. I didn't do fancy holidays or have a second home; it was all about the family and getting ahead. Most of my peers had very different lives and good for them, but that wasn't my reality.

I found this WhatsApp group to be an unhealthy, competitive forum for posting the best pictures from the weekend, holidays, horse-riding, fancy restaurants, etc. One bank holiday, me and the family were out at a farm with the kids. I asked my wife would she take a pic of me, and I was asking her to frame the shot in a particular way to capture the panorama of the countryside.

My wife looked at me... *What are you doing?* She knew I was allergic to photos, so couldn't understand who this pouting man was asking her to do a photoshoot.

What *was* I doing?

I had been made to feel so inadequate, so insecure I was desperately trying to fit in, but I just hadn't realised it. FFS. This wasn't me.

As we drove back with the kids excitedly chirping in the backseat, I was brewing on what I'd allowed to happen. I couldn't compromise on who I was, my values, my essence, just to fit in. As soon as I got home, I left that WhatsApp group. I told my wife, and she said I couldn't just leave like that! I didn't understand why. Sure enough, the individual who had set up the group messaged me to ask why I left it, I told them it just wasn't for me, and left it at that. The truth would have been too messy.

Just a few examples, but they all speak to the impact of the organisational environment which had existed before I joined. An environment

148

cultivated and curated by people in their own likeness.

This wasn't a syndrome I was suffering from.

Once I had this realisation, I started to speak about it. From 2020 onwards I did a lot of public speaking which was about lifting others, whether that was with charities, the wider civil service or even serving police officers. Whenever I gave my own take on the fallacy of imposter syndrome, it got such a strong reception. There was always a penny drop moment with the audience, and I enjoyed watching their faces when it landed. The reaction was amazing from ethnically diverse audiences.

My views on Imposter Syndrome developed through my own experiences, and although my view was in the minority, there is now a growing body of work which is challenging the orthodoxy of this damaging ideology. Interestingly it's grown as more people of colour have entered the debate. There now seems to be a shared view that Imposter Syndrome is damaging, and it is actually systemic discrimination and bias that need to be addressed. From Harvard Business

Review[31], to academics such as Jennifer Jordan[32], there is a rising voice challenging the oppressive orthodoxy of this lie.

And that's what I went to end on, that Imposter Syndrome is a lie.

Once I had accepted this, I was secure enough mentally in my footing within my organisation to take on my biggest challenge yet, dealing with the Met.

---

[31] https://hbr.org/2021/02/stop-telling-women-they-have-imposter-syndrome
[32] https://www.imd.org/research-knowledge/diversity-and-equity-and-inclusion/articles/contextualizing-the-impostor-syndrome/#:~:text=This%20line%20of%20research%20therefore,impostors%E2%80%9D%20when%20in%20those%20institutions.

Chapter 5
Smiles and coat-stands

"I am ashamed to think how easily we capitulate to badges and names, to large societies and dead institutions."

Ralph Waldo Emerson

"What would you do Sal, if I walked over to the corner of the room, picked up that coat-stand and started to smash your head in with it?".

He paused.

He lent back slightly in his chair with a creeping smile, waiting and watching for my response. It was 2019 and my first face to face encounter with one of the senior Met Commanders. It was also my first meeting at New Scotland Yard, a building steeped in history and the main corporate headquarters for the Metropolitan Police Service. New Scotland Yard sits on the bank of the River Thames, a stone's throw from the heart of Government. A shiny, triangular sign marks the entrance, rotating for passersby and gracing the TV screens of homes across the country anytime a case in the capital hits the headlines.

It's a world-famous landmark, and, I'll be honest, as a boy from Kilmarnock I was nervous walking in there. I had to restrain myself from getting my phone out there and then to take a selfie to mark the occasion. Eventually, going there would become part of the humdrum routine, but this was my first time.

They say don't judge a book by its cover. I soon learned that you shouldn't judge a building by its frontage, either. I walked inside, and to my surprise, it was wall to wall beige. They never get that detail right in TV dramas. Based on what I'd watched I'd expected white, grey, and clinical, high-tech even with an air of sophistication. Instead, it was beige in appearance and as I'd later discover, beige in its thinking.

It was noticeable that the majority of the security staff working on the ground floor were people of colour. I stepped into the lift and as the floors rose the ethnicity began to fade away as the seniority of rank increased, literally with each passing floor the building got whiter. By the time I'd get off the lift I was *always* the most senior person of colour in that room. More often than not, the only one in the room.

Why the emphasis on this point?

Because this is in the heart of London, a city in which 46.2%[33] of the population identify as Black. Asian, mixed, or from another ethnic group.

The lack of diversity here was striking.

I was taken aback by what he'd just said. The attempted intimidation was clear.

Before his interlude, we'd been having a discussion about a number of his officers who, in their dealings with the public, had used force.

The use of force in policing is always a contentious issue, and as the person overseeing all cases of police misconduct in London at that

---

[33] https://www.ethnicity-facts-figures.service.gov.uk/uk-population-by-ethnicity/national-and-regional-populations/regional-ethnic-diversity/latest

time, I spoke about it from a particular angle of regulatory oversight. Something I said, or maybe it was the fact I was saying it, clearly rankled with him. Of course, it was just me and him in the room. His analogy could easily be explained away and brushed under the carpet, and he clearly knew that.

I looked at him, I could feel my blood rising, I was back behind my dad's shop counter with some arsehole testing me, threatening me. I mentally sized up whether or not I could take him…. then, I caught myself.

I replied immediately:

"Well, I'd obviously fully defend myself to the extent the law allowed me, I wouldn't run anywhere."

And I smiled.

What I had really wanted to say was, *"you could fuckin try ya arrogant wee bastard."* Instead, I chose to kill him with kindness, demonstrating my defiance with calm and composure to his bully-boy tactics. I watched him shake off the flicker of annoyance that had suddenly etched itself on his face. The conversation moved on.

In this context, it's worth reiterating, my role at the time meant I led the team who investigated the very worst cases of police misconduct in the Met. I was the person who had regulatory oversight of his force, the person who understood *exactly* the sort of behaviour which could equate to misconduct, and yet, he still felt comfortable enough to act like that.
I still find his level of arrogance mind-blowing, even now.

Walking out, just two months into the job, the sense of anticipation I had felt as I entered New Scotland Yard had been replaced with disillusion, and I didn't bother getting that selfie. Instead, as I headed home, I realised that the show of arrogance I had just witnessed wasn't going to be one-off.

And I was right.

A year later, I was well versed in my professional interactions with the Met. There were two common denominators that were a consistent undertone: institutional arrogance and a bewildering sense of denial.

That being said, I don't for one minute wish to tar every officer in the Met with the same brush.

That's a reductive mindset that I know only too well is dangerous and unhelpful. Despite the many issues being faced by the Met and the officers who shape it, it wasn't something I necessarily found with those on the front-line. Instead, it was an issue that reared its head with the more senior ranking officers based at New Scotland Yard.

There was a marked difference.

I've noticed the tendency to paint these two points as binary positions, but I don't see it in that way. I believe it is possible to hold two truths at once here.

Originally, I had taken those attitudes personally, but I shouldn't have. This was who the Met were, long before I was in post. And it wasn't just me who had been left with a bitter taste in their mouth, in dealing with this force. On taking-up my post, I remember one person pulling me aside, someone who had dealt with the Met for many years. Firmly and with ferocity they said, *"The Met, they lie to your face."* Even at the time I was struck by *how* they had said this, as much as what they were saying.

Nevertheless, I carried the point about my independence fiercely and I was going to take the Met and its officers as I found them, conducting myself the right way, without fear or favour.

In 2019, I had my first conversation about stop & search[34]. As policing tactics go, stop and search is arguably the most contentious and challenging issue at the intersection of race and policing, particularly for Black communities. Harmful stereotypes and the subsequent disproportionality and bias these bring are issues that have plagued Black communities for decades, right back to the Windrush generation and the Sus laws that were misused to harass them.

Sus laws

'Sus laws' were created as part of the 1824 Vagrancy Act - at a time of widespread unemployment and poverty. The term 'sus' derived from "suspected person" and, the law gave officers the power to stop, search and even arrest anyone they deemed suspicious - or of 'loitering with the intent to commit an

---

[34] https://www.gov.uk/police-powers-to-stop-and-search-your-rights

> *arrestable offence' - to give the technical answer.*
>
> *With a discretion this broad it systemically created considerable room for bias, and error. It effectively gave the police complete freedom to arrest who they wanted to, when they wanted to.*
>
> *When prosecuting under the sus law, you didn't need to prove that a criminal offence had actually taken place. All that did need to be proven was that the accused had acted suspiciously, and that they had done something to constitute 'loitering with intent'.*

Sus laws opened the floodgates to the disproportionality we still see today. They enabled marginalised communities to become over-policed and under protected, widening the confidence gap between policing and Black communities and embedding an 'us and them' mentality that can only come from years of oppression, and neglect.

Hugh Boatswain, an activist and poet from Hackney said: *"The problem with sus for us was that it was your word versus whoever arrested you… it was enough simply to be Black and in the wrong place at the wrong time".*

In 1981, the whole country was blighted by recession. Brixton, and the local African-Caribbean community in particular, was an area affected, and arguably neglected more than most. High levels of unemployment, poor housing, and statistically[35] a higher crime rate left the area in a state of serious urban decay and social deprivation.

Trust between communities and the police service was, at best, fractured.
On 18 January 1981, a fire broke out at a house party, in New Cross, South-East London. As a result of the fire, 13 young, Black people were killed, aged between 14 and 22. One survivor killed himself two years later.

Authorities working on behalf of the Metropolitan Police stated that the fire had been started inside the property and delivered open verdicts.

Communities believed it was arson, most likely a

---

[35] One could (and I do) argue that the over-policing of such communities renders statistics on crime levels/detection null and void - a concept that could fill a book of its own.

firebomb attack, and blasted the police investigation as a cover-up.

Following on from the fire, a New Cross Massacre Action Committee (NCMAC) was set up, chaired by John La Rose. NCMAC organised a "Black People's Day of Action", later described as 'the largest Black demonstration' in British history. It took place on 2 March 1981 and saw 20,000 people marching through London in unity with the victims, and their families. Beginning in New Cross, the crowd filed past the scene of the fire, 439 New Cross Road, heading towards Hyde Park via Fleet Street and the Houses of Parliament. Those marching then delivered letters to the then Prime Minister, Margaret Thatcher, Scotland Yard, and the Metropolitan Commissioner to acknowledge and address the visible indifference to the 13 deaths. The day was largely misreported, with the Press Council later confirming that The Sun's coverage in particular, was 'damaging to good race relations'.

And it wasn't just the press.

If fractured before, relations between communities and the Met were now at absolute breaking point. And then, they broke entirely.

Operation Swamp, which started on 6 April and was due to finish on 11 April, was the final straw. 'Operation Swamp' was a 10-day police exercise, organised by the Metropolitan Police Service. It set to have 100 plain-clothes officers patrolling 'certain' areas, between 2pm and 11pm, daily. The fact that the word 'swamp' was chosen to label the Op is telling. Two days in, riots erupted across Brixton which are now better known as the 'Brixton uprising'.

Fighting took place between protestors and the Metropolitan Police for three days, with buildings and cars left in a blazing inferno. More than 300 people were injured and the estimated cost of damage was £7.5 million. The riots harnessed widespread media attention, with Blitz-like scenes covering the front-pages and showing the consequence of pent-up, decades-long frustration. The main riot on 11 April was dubbed "Bloody Saturday", with reports suggesting that up to 5,000 people were involved.

It was a watershed moment for race-relations. The then Thatcher Government commissioned an inquiry into the riots and what had led to them which was conducted by Lord Scarman, a lawyer and barrister. This led to the Scarman report[36], which highlighted problems of racial disadvantage and inner-city decline. It warned that urgent action was needed to prevent racial disadvantage becoming an "*endemic, ineradicable disease threatening the very survival of our society*".

Within this report, Scarman also found unquestionable evidence of the disproportionate and indiscriminate use of 'stop and search' powers by the police against black people. David Michael, the first black police officer to serve in Lewisham in the 1970s, described the force as behaving like an "*occupying army*"[37]. Given this history and the issues still being presented around disproportionality and bias, and the confidence gap that still remained between Black communities and the police service, stop and search was something I had to address with the Met.

---

[36] https://onlinelibrary.wiley.com/doi/abs/10.1002/9781118663202.wberen102

[37] https://www.theguardian.com/world/2021/jan/17/forty-years-on-from-the-new-cross-fire-what-has-changed-for-black-briton

UK policing is based on the often-quoted Peelian[38] ideology that to police effectively, you

 must police by consent. Intrinsic to that is the consent, and the subsequent confidence of *all* communities, not just *some* of them. Effective policing lay at the very heart of my role and was the reason I was there in the first place. However, as I delved into that conversation, it soon became apparent that the Met weren't interested.

I had some anecdotal evidence waved in front of me about the link between upping stop and searches and a corresponding drop in knife crime. Not from a study, or any plausible research necessarily, just a senior officer *telling* me that was the case. So, I tried to pitch the conversation in a manner that might speak to the engrained narcissism in the Met, its image. I raised that the indiscriminate use of this power actually caused harm to the force and its reputation, but that wasn't enough. Nope, this is simply what the Met had always done and, still did, and would continue to do. He then

---

[38] https://lordslibrary.parliament.uk/police-standards-and-culture-restoring-public-trust/#:~:text=The%20Peelian%20principles%20said%20officers,and%20secure%20law%20and%20order.

essentially patted me on my head and sent me on my way.

That experience showed me that the notion I'd had about working collegiately on these issues just wasn't going to work. Soft diplomacy was lost on the Met. I realised they were going to have to be dragged to the table, but I just wasn't sure how I would go about doing that.

Something I noticed in my conversations with this, and many other senior officers was a particular pattern of behaviour that followed any difficult, touchy conversation. I'd begun to notice that the conversation would be very one-way. I'd be talking extensively, and they would remain intractably silent, a 'look' frosting over their faces. It was an intense look and felt oddly familiar. It was only after I'd seen it several times that I realised it reminded me of a jedi, using their mind trick.

For the non-Star-Wars fans, if there is such a thing, this is when an expert practitioner of the ever present 'force' (a jedi) is able to manipulate weak-minded individuals through the power of their telepathic suggestions. When they do this in the films, they have that same intense expression, where they are willing the antagonist into their bidding. This jedi mind trick was used by senior officers as a matter of routine, and it was incredibly frustrating. They'd say nothing, let me talk myself out, end on a banality and the conversation would eventually be moved on.

Once I realised this was a deliberate device they used to keep me at arm's length, I wasn't having it.

The conversations being had were about the most serious, sensitive, independent investigations and matters critical to public confidence in their force. I couldn't shy away from that, and neither could they. Instead, as soon as it became apparent they were using the jedi-mind trick, I'd stop talking and ask a direct question:

"What do you think?"

I'd then wait, temptation rising to fill the silence with something, anything…

… but I didn't.

During this standoff, I'd force them to address the point I was making, in a way which they clearly didn't appreciate. They weren't used to it. A lot of that I think comes down to the command-and-control structure of policing. It is *incredibly* hierarchical and not too dissimilar to the military.

To demonstrate this, see below a list of roles which maps out the rank structure of the Metropolitan Police service, specifically.

Rank Structure of the Metropolitan Police

- *Commissioner*
- *Deputy Commissioner*
- *Assistant Commissioner*
- *Deputy Assistant Commissioner*
- *Commander*
- *Chief Superintendent*
- *Superintendent*
- *Chief Inspector*
- *Inspector*
- *Sergeant*
- *Constable*
- *Probationary Police Officer*

The hierarchy that surrounds these ranks is tangible in situ. When meeting senior officers, I'd be introduced to *"Sir"* or *"Ma'am"* by a staff officer. I would pointedly address this senior officer by their first name, making a clear distinction straight off the bat. I was independent, I was non-policing, and I was *not* part of that command-and-control structure. Much like the military, senior officers in policing are treated in a very particular way, something that is instilled in staff and officers from the day they join the service. It also meant that senior officers very rarely heard the word 'no'.

However, being independent meant asserting that independence without fear or favour.

Saying no, where needed, was both powerful and necessary.

The Met definitely weren't used to hearing 'no' from the IOPC, so when I didn't nod along and acquiesce to something, it always provoked a petulant response. An uncomfortable truth I learned was that I was largely alone in my approach. At the most senior levels within the IOPC, people were cowed by the Met. Why?

Because ultimately, I believe they were afraid of them, their power and influence cast a significant shadow.

It's a really damning thing to write, but that was the reality as I saw it.

The Met took the view that the rules which applied to other forces didn't apply to them. Why? Because they weren't just any old police force, they were 'the Met'. I wasn't pandering to that. It was my job and fundamentally I was right to check processes within the force that compromises a third of the police officers in England & Wales. If the Met were used to getting preferential treatment from the IOPC, they wouldn't get it from me.

To be very clear, I'm not alleging that they interfered with our investigations, there is a huge amount of legality wrapped around independent investigations, but it was in other ways, outside of the legislation.

Deadlines? What deadlines?

Rules laid out in the statute requiring the provision of information? Don't think so.

On one occasion, in a highly sensitive, significant investigation, I lost patience due to the endless prevarication by the Met. They just would not provide my team with the information they had asked for that was relevant to our investigation. I said I wanted to pursue it legally to force them to hand this over. Information which we were legally entitled to.

My own organisation was unacquainted with this radical idea of actually using the IOPC's regulatory powers in relation to the Met. That is, challenge them in court, which was what I was going to do if this information wasn't now provided. That one went all the way to the Commissioner.

Interestingly, once the seriousness of my intention had reached that point, within a fortnight my team received all of the outstanding information.

Press releases were hugely contentious and became a real battleground, because there is nothing the Met will defend as fiercely as their brand. This was the hill the Met would die on; image and brand were everything.

When the IOPC independently investigated a case, we would legally take the lead on anything relating to the media. The Met couldn't issue any press lines without it being checked by our own, in-house press office. At critical junctures of the investigation, we would issue media updates and run these past the Met to check for factual accuracy only, but the Met didn't like that. They would use this opportunity to try and edit our release to what they thought it *should* say. Their preference, however, had nothing to do with it. Outside of any factual inaccuracy I would always reject any amendments made by the Met, our independence was everything here.

They hated it.

I mean, they really fucking hated it.

The general pattern would be as follows; the Met would call me to "discuss their concerns", or let's be honest to lean on me. They'd soon realise that wouldn't work and would then escalate to the level above me. I would then have to deal with the insipid weakness of certain senior IOPC management flapping to the point where I'd be asked to change *something/anything* which could be then used as a sop to appease the Met. But where did appeasement get you?

As it was my decision I wouldn't budge, and I always had the grounds to back it up.

It got to the point that we'd argue over words, pointless mindless details that wasted time and resources. It was another hidden way the Met skillfully exercised its power to try and get what it had always been accustomed to getting. It was a real eye-opener for me, and on many occasions highlighted to me that the Met could and would use every tactic to get what they wanted. They were skillful at it; they were masters at it. This is probably where my broken flight or fight response came in handy.

But it wasn't just me, I knew other police forces disliked the way the Met conducted themselves and how their scandals brought them into collateral disrepute - not that it was ever voiced openly. Why? Because the Met had significant influence at a national level, and forces looked to them for leadership on initiatives, especially given that they had a budget far beyond the reach of others.

On one occasion, I attended firearms training with a colleague. It took place at the location where Sergeant Angle, I mean Angel, received his riot training in Hot Fuzz. I got to see a whole range of things, from firing a taser, to seeing a stun grenade being deployed, to firing a whole range of state-of-the-art firearms. It was the double-barrel shotgun which made the biggest impression on me, literally. The kick from it was so fierce it left me with a massive bruise on my arm, and the concrete block I had aimed at was pretty much disintegrated.

I saw up close and personal just how extensive the training is for firearms officers on the ground and left feeling hugely impressed at the level of training these officers received.

Now of course, when making my decisions on whether officers had acted appropriately or not, it was absolutely imperative that I had a solid understanding of operational policing, including how firearms officers operate. But I couldn't shake the feeling that there was always another agenda at play. An agenda in which by getting the VIP treatment, I'd be dazzled by just how great the Met were.

The more invitations I accepted, the more that feeling just would not shake. I was acutely aware that the razzamatazz of such experiences could be incredibly seductive, and at worst, could allow a person to totally lose sight of *why* they were actually there. In technical terms, it could lead to those working at the opposite end of the table to become the victims of 'regulatory capture'. When working on behalf of an independent body, that simply was not an option.

Regulatory Capture

Regulatory capture is an economic theory that was introduced to the world in the 1970s by the late George Stigler, a Nobel laureate economist at the University of Chicago. It means when regulatory agencies may come to be dominated by the industries or interests, they are charged with regulating. The result is that an agency, charged with acting in the public interest, instead acts in ways that benefit incumbent firms in the industry it is supposed to be regulating.

In my response to any such invitation, and my demeanour when in attendance, I quite deliberately made it clear that this would absolutely not work with me. It would not change my approach, it would not change my method, and it would not change any outcome.

And guess what?

I stopped getting invitations from the Met.

As I think about this now through a reflective lens, particularly as I write this book, I realise the Met for me was the bloated bearded officer I saw as a terrified wee boy, swilling lager from a can in the back of my dad's shop. Caught red-handed and yet still arrogant enough to dismiss me with a satisfied smile, silencing me with that well practiced finger to its lips.

Despite the challenges, I created a decent working relationship with many of those in senior positions. Even those at New Scotland Yard, despite initial impressions. This, I believe, was as a result of my principled approach, and my insistence on setting boundaries.

Boundaries help you define what you are comfortable with, what you are *not* comfortable with, and how you expect to be treated. Establishing these boundaries was, and always is important, in any walk of life. Whether that be at home, in relationships, or at work. It often takes courage to set boundaries in the first place, because it's likely that if you need to, you're already being tested. Not everyone will respect it, but don't let that dissuade you.

The Met would continually test my boundaries. Being values-led meant that I always went back to my core, my true north. Compromising my key principles was never an option.

Then, 2020 happened. Covid happened. George Floyd happened. Black Lives Matter rang through the ears of the world. Police accountability became a global news story.

Little did I know then, just how much my own life would change as a result.

www.truenorth-thebook.com

Chapter 6

Dad

"I used to think grief was this linear thing that you limped through. Pass one section and onto the next - a box ticking exercise for the broken hearted. But it isn't like that at all. The landscape of grief is complicated. It can change from one day to another, and will look different, for everyone."

Sal Naseem, 2023

Krispy Kreme doughnuts, the sticky, sweet American treats that are so ridiculously calorific and raised the threshold for what's socially acceptable to spend on a doughnut. The originators of all the deluxe flavours, from original glaze to lotus biscoff, and lemon cheesecake and many more varieties.

But for me, the sight of a Krispy Kreme doughnut turns my stomach.

On the 23rd of February 2020, I'd filled a trolley
from bottom to top with dozens of the things.
With the speed of a frenzied sugar addict and
my mind on total autopilot.

My beloved Dad had just passed away, after a
grueling, painful three years - for him, and for us.

I'd put one step shakily in front of the other,
heading straight for the local supermarket with
my wife and filling the cart with anything glazed I
could get my hands on. How else to thank the
doctors and nurses who had single-handedly
kept my dad, and us, going for as long as they
did?

The Scottish way, calories.

In the three years previous, Dad's health had
deteriorated rapidly.

For three years, he was in and out of hospital,
me the emergency contact for both him and
Mum, ready and waiting to hit the M6 any time
the phone rang.

For three years, this degenerative neurological disease slowly took him from us, piece by piece, in real time and in front of our very eyes.

For three years, I was numb, living in survival mode and doing anything but.

At the time, I was living in Birmingham and my parents were still in Kilmarnock. Initially, although very poorly, for the majority of the time my dad was still at home, and still working in the shop he'd so lovingly built from the ground up.

Now and again, things would take a turn, something would happen, and the phone would ring. Day or night, I'd pack up my bag and hit the motorway. All 350 miles of it. At best, it was five or six hours of time to think and reflect, and that was on a good day. Some days the weather could, and often did make my life that bit more difficult. Over that three-year period, I think I saw every kind of rain. I'm Scottish, I know rain but when your eyes are burning, and your mind is full of worst-case scenarios, that rain hits differently.

I remember one particular night there was a storm, right in time for the emergency dash to

Scotland. I had to go; Dad had been taken into hospital. It was one of those storms that hit the threshold to be given a specific name, but I can't remember what it was called now. Travel warnings loomed and as the weather worsened, I silenced the voice inside me that said this wasn't my safest, most sensible hour. Minutes after I passed the border to enter Scotland, the motorway closed right behind me. But I kept on driving until I reached the gate that led to Mum and Dad's, the metaphorical light at the end of a long, rain-lashed tunnel.

Back at home were my wife and children, and the full-time job I was holding down to keep a roof over their heads. It was a lot to manage, but, as anyone who's faced challenge will tell you, you always find the strength to deal with it at the time. It's in retrospect that you struggle to understand just how that was mined.

Mentally, I was just about holding it together, keeping too busy to break. Physically, the weight piled on as I stress-ate, shoving sugary snacks down my neck to power me through the long days and lonely drives. While the waistline had seen better days, career wise, it was a pretty positive time for me. After years of challenge and setbacks, I'd just secured the job as interim

Regional Director for London, at the
Independent Office for Police Conduct. An
important position that I accepted with respect,
and dedication.

As I've mentioned, as part of my role it was my
job to oversee the most serious and sensitive
cases of police misconduct, across every force
in London. This included, British Transport
Police, the City of London Police, and the Met.

Alongside my home in Birmingham and my
parent's in Scotland, it meant spinning a lot of
plates. One minute, I'd be talking stop and
search with some of the country's most senior
police officers and the next, I'd be asking a
consultant what my dad's prognosis was, the
good news getting more and more scarce.

As Dad's health got worse, he spent more and
more time in hospital. As the emergency calls
became more frequent, I settled into a routine
that before long was as familiar as any other.

Get in the car, panic.

Conquer the drive, try to settle.

Go through the barrier, take a ticket and park up, and *never* in daylight. In the dark, always.

Then, I'd take the path across the car park and make my way to the ward that was fast becoming my second home.

One thing that is etched in my memory are the paintings that hung in the main hospital corridor, just before you turned into the maze of subsidiary corridors.

I love art, I've always loved art, both to view and to practice. The paintings were always some form of landscapes which tied to the area. Occasionally I'd stop in my tracks as I squinted at the paintings, trying to place if I knew that location. The paintings that hung in that particular corridor were beautiful punctuations of colour, craft, and care on some of my darkest days.

They were all by local artists, and all for sale, with the proceeds going towards the upkeep of a hospital that, like all others, felt tired and dated. As the months stretched on, people (who like me had taken comfort in the artwork), snapped them up and took them away from the hospital, home.

I'd like to think as a reminder of what they'd got through, and how the small things really are the most important.

New paintings would adorn the walls and soon, the cycle would begin again.

As much as I loved the artwork, I never bought any. The only precious thing I wanted to take home from that building was my dad. But I couldn't. And so, I'd push through the double doors to Ward 3B, the green vinyl flooring squeaking under the work shoes that I hadn't had time to change, the smell of anti-bac and cleaning solution filling my nose and reminding me just where I was.

If the smell didn't do that, the sounds would. The incessant screech of machines beeping, ricocheting throughout the place until, after a while, you just didn't hear it anymore. I quietly struggle to enter a hospital these days. But all too quick, I was up there every other weekend.

Dad largely in hospital, me and Mum muddled together the best we could, doing what we had to do to look after Dad and each other. Sometimes, that was as simple as me hoovering and tidying the house, grabbing bits from the supermarket for the fridge and cupboards so that Mum had one less thing to worry about. Not that she ever let me feel or see the strain she so definitely would have been under. They say tough times bring out the strength in people and Mum, unsurprisingly, was incredible. She managed what I can only describe as a regime of medication with precision, and love. The love that I had been fortunate enough to grow up around and witness between them. That love was as apparent in the hospital as it had been growing up, and the environment did nothing to change that with Mum, or anyone else for that matter.

Dad had soon settled and become part of the metaphorical furniture, making friends with the other patients and the doctors and nurses who so lovingly took care of him. By the end, I was on first name terms with the team, and they knew him, the family, and all about us. My Dad made sure of it.

He'd sit in bed, the ever-proud Father, sharing stories with anyone who would listen about the job I was doing and the cases I'd been working on. It was a beautiful thing, and despite all else I'll be forever grateful that we had that.

But it was *hard*, and visiting Dad was always bittersweet. Every time I visited; I could see that piece by piece this fucking awful illness was just taking him. Chipping away at him until my role model, my hero, this kind man was disappearing right in front of me.

Being the man he was, he didn't take that lying down, and despite his health, he didn't want to retire. The shop and everything that came with it was all he knew, and he loved it. He was the community, and the community was him. He fought the very notion of retiring until eventually, the choice was taken from him, breaking his heart in the process, and ours.

The shop was sold, and the day before the keys needed to be handed over, I spent the hours sorting through everything that needed to be cleared, to make way for the new vendors who would take the baton from my dad. I spent the day packing my dad's life's work into 30 odd bin bags, closing the door on 35 years of hard graft, happy memories, and unshakable dedication. All I could do was be there with him and make it as easy a process as possible. Of course, it felt anything but easy, it was torture, and yet, the hardest was still to come.

The illness and its symptoms were incredibly cruel. One by one, Dad's senses in their most basic form were taken from him. Initially, it was his hearing that was badly affected. He had special supersonic ear devices that meant he could just about hear us if we shouted, but his sight was also getting increasingly poor.

Initially, he lost his sight in one eye, consultants telling us that he would lose his sight in his other eye almost definitely. Me and Mum would underplay how serious things were looking, keeping updates like that to ourselves very deliberately. He'd shielded us for our whole lives, and it was our turn to shield him. We needed to protect him from the cruelty that was his illness in whichever way we could, and I don't have any regrets about that.

On the surface, I stayed strong for Mum, and Dad. I had to. Internally? It was destroying me, too. It was horrible. It was single handedly the worst thing I've ever experienced.

By the end, Dad was completely bed-bound, he could barely walk. As anyone who has had a relative in hospital for a long period of time will know, lying down all day is not good for the mind, or the body. It takes a team of people to keep your loved one comfortable, including the visitors that each day roll in to lift the spirits of the person they're coming to see, their own in absolute tatters.

One of the last things I ever did for my dad was massage his feet and ankles to take down the swelling that had taken a grip. Lying down will do that to a person, and it looked painful. Anything I could do to help make him more comfortable. Once he was settled, I fed him his dinner, the choice of which we'd picked in the morning from the ward staff, as we did every day. It was vegetable soup that day. Then, like every evening, I'd gone home, updating my family on the day we'd had and preparing myself for another day of the same.

And then, the phone rang.

What followed was an out of body experience.

Dark room.
Blue walls.
Me, sitting opposite a consultant.

I remember the setting because it felt all-encompassing at the time, the colours loud, somehow.

The content of that meeting? I couldn't tell you. All I remember is the consultant telling me that my dad didn't have much longer left, and that it was time to let the people that needed to know and know quickly.

I hadn't known it at the time, but I'd just fed Dad his last meal.

The staff on shift didn't think my dad would survive the night, but, with his typical tenacity he did. He waited until everyone was around him. Me, Mum, my wife, and my siblings were all with him as he passed peacefully. That's a blessing that on the harder days, I hold onto. When you lose someone you love, those blessings are a lifeline. The fact that we all got to be there, to say goodbye, not everyone gets to do that.

After that? A total blur. Stumbling through the hospital exit, everything around me seemed hazy, like walking through fog. The world carrying on around you while your world has been turned upside down and stopped, nothing making any sense. You go through the motions, getting in the car, putting the key in the ignition, catching your eye in the rear-view mirror, tear soaked and bloodshot. Had what I'd dreaded for as long as I can remember, actually just happened?

Once back inside the house, in what felt like slow motion I'd started to climb the stairs, gripping the banister, one step at a time. Once I reached the top, I went into the bedroom and collapsed on the floor. I opened my mouth and all I remember is a noise, this horrible animalistic wail pouring its way out of me. I couldn't stop. Months, no years of pain, suffering and deep stabbing sorrow spilling out of me uncontrollably. I don't think I could have stopped it if I'd tried. I remember my wife holding me, I don't know for how long, but it was a while.

In my faith, it's tradition to bury those who have passed as soon as possible, and so, before I'd had time to even process what had happened, we were having my dad's funeral, the day after he'd passed. Thankfully, Dad's friends from his mosque organised everything. They were *amazing*.

I was a mess. A total shell, broken and absolutely exhausted from the relentless trauma of it all.

The day itself was a cold, winter's day, fitting for the scene and how the world around me felt at the time. I was freezing, absolutely cold through. You know when nothing can warm you? I remember shaking, violently shaking, was it the cold, or the emotion? I don't know, perhaps both. I vividly remember my youngest son, taking my hand and holding it. He held my hand all day, supporting *his* dad, as *he* said goodbye to his own.

The mosque was rammed. Members of our family, the community, even some of the nurses came to pay their respects. The special constable who I mentioned earlier in this book? He came along to say goodbye to Dad. At the time I was too broken to even register, but looking back now the sendoff my dad was given was a testament to the impact he had on every single person he met. Despite our challenges when first moving to Kilmarnock, no matter the lifestyle, creed or the colour, he *loved*, and was loved by them all just as much.

Within a few days, I was back at work. There was no phased return, I came back in full *beast* mode, throwing myself into work in a way that would tire me now, just thinking about it.

This was in no way by accident. Keeping busy had been the antidote to three years of slow, painful torture and, so, keeping busy was the tool I decided to use to mask the fact that inside, I was destroyed. In the job I did, I was used to viewing difficult, sensitive content. But let in the images of my dad in his last days? No way. Too horrific. Work became my best friend, a welcome distraction from the trauma I was trying so hard to bury.

Every day was work.

Go to work, complete the work and then find a bit more work for good measure. Need something doing? Sal's your guy. No days off, no limits.

Every now and then I would take myself into a room and just cry, a muffled, silent scream. Once I was level, I'd carry on, back to work. Most people didn't know what had happened because I didn't tell many people. I don't think anyone would have guessed, either. That I'd just lost my dad, one of the most precious people I'd ever known. My results wouldn't have hinted at any heartache, either. I was smashing it, throwing myself into anything that I could. I crammed about three years' worth of experience into one year. The minute I got home and had time to think? The thoughts would spin and the PTSD that I was undoubtedly suffering from would rear its head.

One memory of Dad just wouldn't leave me. It was in his last few weeks in hospital, and he had to go to the bathroom, his spirit was so strong he wanted to go by himself so with the nurse's help he got up and walked with the help of a Zimmer-frame to get there. I had just come into the ward and seen as he came out of the bathroom heading back to his bed. He was shuffling, he couldn't walk. He looked up at me, and he gave this look which said everything while he didn't say anything. It's a memory that's still very difficult to write about because it was a moment shared between the two of us, unspoken. I felt his pain and we both just knew what was going to happen.

The look my dad gave me, his expression, that memory was something that tortured me. So, I retreated to my toxic safety mechanism, to drown this out with the safety net of so much work so I couldn't think of him.

You'll know from earlier chapters that I grew up in a place riddled with addiction and the misery that surrounds it. During this period, I got it. For the first time, I sympathised with the "junkies" I'd so badly despised years earlier. I can now understand that people get to a point where they fall into an abyss and resort to whatever they need to, to numb the pain that's tearing them apart more than any drug ever could.

These thoughts alone, even in my distorted mind at the time, were worrying. More worrying was how I showed up/or didn't, at home. I was failing as a father, and a husband, the most important job I have ever and will ever have. The only job title in the world that will *ever* mean a thing to me. I should have been at my best for my family, and I wasn't, I couldn't. I felt like a bastard. I was letting them down, myself down, my dad down. I knew I wasn't being who I needed to be for them.

During that time, ironically the work that I did is some of the work I'm most proud of. I would like to think that the impact the work had will be felt for many, still today. But so what? What did it mean if I wasn't fulfilling my role as a husband, or a father?

While a distraction, work was preventing me from dealing with what had actually happened, not just in my dad's passing, but in the three years that had led to it. I needed to confront that to be better for the people who so badly needed me, and who I needed in equal measure. And so, I decided to speak to someone - a counsellor who, while lovely, I met with extreme scepticism. I just didn't buy it at all. How was speaking to someone about the horror I'd gone through going to help? Bringing all of that suffering to the surface? How could that possibly help *anyone*?

But, in time, thankfully I was proven wrong.

Talking to a counsellor meant I could talk about things that I couldn't speak to other people about - not without traumatising them in the process. I could pull my deepest, darkest thoughts from beneath the weight that I'd buried them and release them to a person who could actually help me to process it all. Once I realised that, it was like a dam that broke. Like the scream that came out of me the night my dad died, once I started I couldn't have stopped it if I'd tried.

Speaking to someone was the first step in actually recovering. Recovering? That's not the right word because you never get over it. An experience like that changes you. How couldn't it? I will never be the same person that I was before those three terrible years. It became obvious to me that those three years were just the warmup. No one knows loneliness like grieving, and that was something I learned very quickly. It became clear to me that the 23rd February 2020 had marked the start of a new battle, a battle with no chance of a truly happy ending. He wasn't coming back.

As I processed the trauma, I still felt unable to talk about him. It was too painful, and my battered heart just couldn't take any more of that. Instead, I *did* a lot to mark his name and make sure that his memory, and legacy lived on. I raised funds for the local mosque, so that they could buy a trolley bed for future funeral services. Anything to thank them for the support they had shown me, my family, and my dad in his life, but also in his death. No words would ever be enough to thank them for what they did for us.

Then, three weeks after he died, I wrote an article for the local newspaper that talked to my dad, and the man that he was. The headline spoke of a 'gentleman Kilmarnock shopkeeper' and was followed by the stories I'd wanted to share with the world about the best person I knew. In tribute to Dad, I would like to share snippets of that article with you, here.

"My dad, Barkat Ali Naseem, was born in poverty 74 years ago.

"Through sheer will he made a life for himself that was rich, not necessarily in material things, but in the positive impact he had on others. My dad was the best person I knew.

"He was the standard of person I aspire to be both personally and professionally. He taught me that character is what you do when no-one is looking".

The article went on to share how my dad had run his Hill Street shop from 1983 up until the year before he passed. It spoke to the fact that he was an electrical engineer by trade, but decided to move to Kilmarnock from Huddersfield, West Yorkshire to carve a new life for his family.

"I know that moving to Kilmarnock and serving the community for nearly 40 years was his great joy.

"He was a true people person and always remembered everyone no matter how long it'd been since he'd seen them, and he always had a smile on his face.

"He was generous to a fault, not just with his family but with anyone in need. We've been overwhelmed with new stories of his generosity following his passing.

Tributes from the community came flooding in. The outpouring of love for him was incredible, healing even. So many tributes came in that the following week, a second piece was published in the national paper, *The Daily Record*.

I never actually knew *how* loved he was until after he died, and I read those tributes. I finally realised just *why* that shop had been so important to him, right up until he died. It wasn't just a shop, or a job, it was who he was. He loved the community, and he was loved in return. The community that in so many ways had been difficult, became intrinsic to who he was.

Within the tributes one overriding theme was clear, that he was a gentleman. A father to four, a Granddad and, above all else, a gentleman, to the end.

Now, I can speak about my dad.

And I do, whenever I get the chance.

I speak about him and the *good* man that he was. How he would *always* do the right thing, even when no one was watching. Just because it was the *right* thing to do.

I speak about the fact that everything I do is for him, and the rest of my wonderful family. He showed me what it means to be a father, a husband, and how to be there for the ones you love.

I speak about the fact that along with a broken heart, he left me with *so* many gifts. My work ethic, my drive, my moral compass. That's all my dad.

I speak to the fact that I could never do a bang average job, at any of the above. Don't get me wrong, I could never be him, he was a one-off. But I am his legacy.

It's been four years now, and still, it feels like yesterday. I will never be able to rationalise the ending my dad had. Such a cruel end for such a kind man. The injustice of it all is just too much. And so, I don't try to rationalise it anymore. I sit with my grief, and I concentrate on being the best tribute to my dad, and my mum that I can be.

Everything I did the year he died was to stay afloat, to drown out the pain. Everything I do now is for him, my Mum, my wonderful wife, and my beautiful children. The work I do is no longer to bury the pain inside me but is a tribute to them, and to him.

It's why I hold myself to such a high standard, and I always will.

Dad

Chapter 7
A summer like no other

*"Out of intense complexities, intense
simplicities emerge."*
Winston Churchill

So here I am.

It's 2019 and personally, my world has been
trashed.
Professionally? Things look a lot brighter.

I'd landed the role as Regional Director for
London, at the Independent Office for Police
Conduct. Despite being on an interim basis at
the time, I was determined to give it everything I
had, in the time that I had. As I mentioned
earlier, as part of the role I was set to become
responsible for *the* most serious and sensitive
cases of police misconduct, across every police
force in London. It wasn't lost on me for a
second just how important that role was.

My predecessor, who had sat on the panel that offered me the role, had gone on to fill the role of Deputy Director General. I'd got stuck straight in, as had he, and everything was ticking along quite nicely.

Until it wasn't.

In late 2019, while everything at home was about as bad as it can get, I was sat down by the Deputy Director General, who looked as steely as he did serious.

Oh, shit.

He told me that rumours were circulating regarding inappropriate behaviour between my predecessor and another colleague. It transpired that a relationship had started between the pair, which organisationally, was *technically* fine. People's private lives are their private lives, at the end of the day. But, and there is a significant but, he was married, he was her superior. He didn't disclose the relationship, despite there being a quite clear conflict of interest in the two of them working together, particularly given the nature of our work. This became particularly relevant as the colleague in question was the

Lead Investigator on a highly contentious case at the time.

It didn't look great.

Naturally, news of the relationship and that potential conflict of interest risked huge reputational damage, it set the cat amongst the proverbial internal pigeons.

From my perspective, it wasn't just the reputation of the organisation at stake, but also the credibility of an investigation that was incredibly high profile and had the interest of senior parliamentarians. News of the scandal came as a total shock to me. But then, the more I thought about it, the more that shock subsided. My mind ran over things that I'd seen, things that had *niggled* at me, perhaps even subconsciously. I began to join the dots, and a wider, uncomfortable picture began to take shape.

"How had I missed that?"

The process took its course, as it does in organisations of that size and nature, and eventually - albeit not without pushback, he was dismissed.

At work I keep my head down, I always have done.

I don't network, because I don't know how to, I don't stand by the metaphorical "water cooler" wasting time on gossip, and I don't bother with after-work socials that take time I could be spending with my family. On the surface, I probably come across as pretty boring, but I'm quite happy with that. And so, amongst the shitstorm my predecessor had left me in, I did what I always do, I got my head down and got on with my job.

But the shitstorm hadn't finished with me quite yet. As the weeks went by, one by one, a stream of female investigators began to approach me. They had questions about what these recent developments meant for their role, and importantly, their progression. A common theme soon began to materialise, weaved through the many conversations I had with a cohort of largely female, junior members of staff.

Reading between the lines it became clear that false assurances had been made. Expectations were high, and planned paths to progression were seemingly well cemented. These young women had been made all sorts of promises, some of which were quite frankly bollocks and way above anything that I, him, or anyone else in the organisation could legitimately have guaranteed. I had to navigate these conversations very carefully and honestly, managing expectations and relaying foundations that were built on lies. There is no other word for it.

I remember one young woman sitting with me, the cogs turning at what she was hearing from me: *"He was just the seller of dreams, wasn't he?"*. I nodded and smiled sadly. She was absolutely right, he was. I resisted the temptation to say something stronger.

As I said before, I had noticed things previously. Nothing that posed a safeguarding issue, but things that just didn't seem quite *right*. Given our positions at the time, the meetings we held together were to discuss high profile, sensitive information. These would usually be organised *well* in advance, with careful consideration given to who should and shouldn't be in attendance. At times of crisis, they'd be drawn together quickly, but with the same care and precision in limiting the number of attendees, to mitigate against the risk of information being shared that, at that stage, shouldn't be.

I remember once we'd be walking into one of these meetings, and he'd draped himself over the desk of a junior female investigator and said:

"Hey, why don't you come along?"

It was a small thing, but it niggled.

I'm not someone who often pulls rank, or even thinks much about hierarchy when it's not necessary but, given the nature of those meetings? It wasn't right. Now I have a better awareness of patriarchy, male violence against women and girls and power dynamics in the workplace. When I look back at that now I look at it with a far harsher lens, and it more than niggles.

As I mentioned, the man in question was on the panel of those who had hired me. While working I'd always felt a sense of loyalty to him. Looking back now I don't know why; I got that job through hard work and dedication to the role. But, once all of that came out and the underbelly of what he'd been up to came to light, I lost all respect for him. Any sense of loyalty that I had, it just dissipated.

Despite being new in post, I had no choice but to hit the ground running, at pace. I'd pick things up that were months in the planning and taking place tomorrow, without the luxury of picking up the phone and asking for some sort of steer from the individual who *had* been leading on it. He was long gone. One of those things was a speaking slot, at a conference being hosted by the Police Federation.

For those who aren't in policing, the Police Federation is the staff association that represents all police officers across England and Wales.

Given my role at the time, and the organisation I represented, I knew that I was in for a *tough gig*, and an even tougher crowd.

I walked in, and from the moment I did I could feel that structural tension. I took my seat and settled myself for the onslaught that lay ahead. Looking around, I sized up the audience to see exactly what I was in for. Very White, and *very* male. As I scanned the room further, it dawned on me, I was the only person of colour in the room. Story of my life.

I'd sat myself quite deliberately at the very back of the room, alongside some other IOPC colleagues who, like me, were very conscious of the dynamics in play. Before long it was my time to take the stage. As I headed up to the podium, the crowd erupted. The noise ricocheted off the walls and filled the room. They were actually booing me. Although I took it in my stride, I did hear it. I climbed the steps and made my way towards the compere who, in total fairness (and contrast), gave a perfectly nice introduction. The booing subsided and I was faced with a sea of tension. They really shouldn't have bothered with their cack-handed chorus, I already felt pretty unwelcome, but I suppose the crowd had made their position unequivocal now.

I was the person who represented the independent regulator of policing in England & Wales. And I was absolutely torn to bits as I walked to take the stage. While I'm not saying categorically that it's a race thing, when you take a step back and look at the optics of approx. 400 White men booing the only person of colour in the room…. it's not great, is it?

I took some hard questioning, stood firm and did my thing. I left the stage, boarded the train, and came home to tell my wife what had happened. And that routine continued.

Now I look back, with some of the issues that have reared their ugly heads in the past four years, within the reports that have made so many headlines, it paints a pretty revealing picture when it comes to the Police Federation and the issues that blight policing. Would that happen now? I'd hope not. Could I say hand on heart for *certain* that it wouldn't happen now? No, I couldn't.

Four years is a long time, but the memories of that particular time I think will *always* feel like yesterday. And given the events of 2020, that's no surprise.

2020, what a year.

Still tending to the scars that were the loss of my dad, little did I know that this thing called Covid would soon emerge from the ether and turn the world upside down. I remember hearing the rumblings and thinking nothing of it. One of those moral panics that plasters the front of every newspaper, to become quite literally fish and chip wrapping the next day. When asked by my children what I thought of it, I remember saying quite firmly:

"It's a load of bollocks, it won't amount to anything - just you watch."

That comment didn't age well.

At the time, within my role I was planning an event to bring together young people from marginalised communities, in order to speak about the issues causing most friction and concern. It was set to be a big event, with a lot of money and time being dedicated to ensuring that those in attendance got ample opportunity to speak and be *heard*. The day before the event, given all of the unknowns and risks that came with that, I had to make a call, and we cancelled the event. I was absolutely torn over it.

The week after, the whole country locked down, and then came the surreal experience, which was all things; face masks, anti-bacterial hand gel, clapping on the doorstep and fighting your way through the supermarket to get your hands on toilet rolls.

Alongside all of that, the job continued.

The sort of job I did, it didn't stop. But, luckily for me, I was at home with a laptop. Not like the people who were on the frontline, working for just about minimum wage in what were tough situations at the best of times. We, like everyone, stood on the doorstep and clapped for those heroes. Given what I'd been through, I held those individuals in the highest possible regard already. I can't imagine how hard it must have been for the staff, patients, and families within hospitals, with the added complexity that was Covid.

Quite early on, me and the family actually got Covid. That wasn't pleasant. It was at a time where we knew very little, and scaremongering was at its peak. There was a lot of fear, particularly in the south-Asian community where we had a disproportionate number of fatalities. It was a tough juggle. As a dad, a husband, and a member of the senior leadership team at work, you're trying to make sure you're okay, your family are okay and your team are okay, with everything they need to work at home while staying healthy, and *somehow* sane.

We had a legal duty to continue with investigations, and cases were still coming in thick and fast. Alongside Covid, people were still dying after interactions with the police. The landscape remained in some ways similar, but in other ways, it looked totally different. Multiple lockdowns, police officers not wearing PPE, police officers not being able to *access* PPE, it was all untrodden territory.

Covid laws were widely publicised, but not particularly *well* and, as a result, were not at all well understood. The referral of Boris Johnson, the serving prime minister at the time was a particularly interesting exercise, largely given that all the emails (and therefore evidence), had been deleted. Pretty unhelpful when considering whether an independent investigation was required.

And then, amongst all of the chaos that had taken hold of the globe, something happened that seemed to grind the world to a halt.

9 minutes and 29 seconds.
On the 25th of May 2020, George Floyd was murdered. In 9 minutes, 26 seconds, his life was taken from him, on camera, and the world watched.

One of the four police officers involved in his murder, and I use that word very deliberately, knelt on George's neck for such a long time, and with *such* brutality, that he was starved of oxygen.

His crime? The alleged use of a counterfeit bank note. I use the word alleged very deliberately, too. Footage that played out the entirety of his murder went viral.

9 minutes, 29 seconds of unarguable, unequivocal police brutality, went viral.

9 minutes and 29 seconds made its way into houses worldwide, onto the screens that we'd been glued to in the weeks previous, as covid briefings gave a glimpse of what our lives might look like in the coming weeks.

9 minutes, 29 seconds brought the conversation of race, and racism, to the forefront of conversation. It made a mark on the world that I hope will scar, as a permanent reminder to the horror that is racism.

I never actually watched the footage in its entirety. Not because I didn't care or didn't want to, but because I just couldn't face it.

In making decisions on some of the worst cases of police misconduct in recent history, I've had to watch people's lives being taken on camera, more times than I care to share or think about. No one tells you that when you apply for the job. You know it will be awful, you know you'll feel horrendous afterwards, but you steel yourself. It's an essential part of the job.

I'd led the team looking into the Grenfell Tower fire, to see if there was any police misconduct involved. Reading the phone transcripts of the people trapped in the tower was one of the worst things I've ever had to work on. Reading all of their accounts, their last moments. It's one of the hardest things I've had to do professionally and truthfully, it's never left me.

But still, I just couldn't bring myself to watch that footage.

It was the thought of watching the *knee* of a racist in uniform take away the life of a man in broad daylight, stealing his oxygen with such brute force that the only option he had left was to gasp for air and call for his mother. The thought of it made me feel sick. That footage went global, and I'm glad it did. When something like that is in the public domain, it can't be explained away, and it can't be ignored. As a result, there was accountability for those officers.

On reflection, I think the impact of that video was driven by the circumstances we were in at the time. Don't get me wrong, footage as bad as that would always have made an impact. But, I think it would have been '*just another*' name of a Black man whose life was lost at the hands of the American police service. And that list contains enough names to fill a chapter in this book. People at that point were less distracted, lives were even more rooted in social media and TV because of lockdown, and this weird cocoon amplified the impact of this murder. The story kept growing, with the Black Lives Matter (BLM) movement leading the way in ensuring it stayed alive, keeping George Floyd's name and memory relevant.

Such is the link between BLM and George Floyd, that people often think BLM was created in the *wake* of his death, but it wasn't. Black Lives Matter was founded in 2013 by three Black women; Patrisse Cullors, Alicia Garza and Opal Tometi. They set up the movement in the wake of *another* young Black man's murder, Trayvon Benjamin Martin.

In 2012, while visiting his father's fiancée at her gated community home in Florida, Martin was shot.

His crime? Being Black, in an area that wasn't. He was 17 years old.

The gunman was 28-year-old George Zimmerman, a neighbourhood watch volunteer. BLM was created in response to the acquittal of George Zimmerman. Despite shooting dead a child in broad daylight, for no reason other than being Black and wearing a hoodie, Zimmerman was given the lesser charge of manslaughter.

On May 26, 2020 - the day after George Floyd was murdered, protests took place around the world. It was estimated that between 15 million and 26 million people had participated in the demonstrations in the United States alone, making the protests the largest in US history. Globally, people joined together and took to the streets, calling for reform, equality and above all - justice. The last words of George Floyd became their rallying cry:

"I can't breathe.".

So here I am, Regional Director for London, at the body responsible for police misconduct in England and Wales, at a time when police misconduct is well and truly in the spotlight. Not just at home, but around the world.

As with any large organisation, a team of people are hired specifically to create the content that goes out into the public domain. One by one, organisations were starting to come forward with their view on the event, and the thoughts and feelings it had uncovered. Others were paralysed by fear and said nothing, waiting for the next big headline to come along and brush it all under the carpet. Here's the kicker, we were the latter.

I sat, waiting. When were we going to say something?

In the end, out of sheer frustration, I sent my own message to my team and the people I worked with. I didn't seek permission; it was my own personal viewpoint, and I wasn't prepared to sit on it for any longer. I talked about my own experiences of racism, how I'd had to have 'the chat' with my children about the issues that yet again found themselves on the front pages of the national newspapers. Members of my team, particularly those with lived experience of racism, reached out and thanked me. The colleagues from other teams reached out as well, to say thank you. They didn't need to. I was just doing what any decent human being should do at that time and acknowledging a situation that needed to be acknowledged.

We needed to get out there as an organisation and be visible in the media, but we were paralysed by fear, and the risk aversion which seems to be a sickness that infects too many regulatory bodies. Out of sheer frustration, I took on this role of getting our presence and voice out there in the media, because to me, being independent didn't mean being invisible.

During that period, the number of cases coming in rocketed, particularly those that featured race discrimination. Each and every case was subject to a heightened sense of scrutiny, there was a renewed lens on the issue of racism. That year, I dealt with some of the most high-profile cases of police misconduct seen by policing in recent years.

The stop and search of Bianca Williams and Ricardo Dos Santos, two Black British Olympic athletes, was one of them. (It was also a case that for me would have implications years later).

In July 2020, Bianca Williams and Richardo Dos Santos were stopped by police as they drove to their home in Maida Vale, West London. Travelling with their three-month-old son at the time, footage of a highly distressed Williams began to circulate. While being forced to leave her vehicle in order to be searched, Williams could be seen repeatedly telling police that her son was in the car. She was distraught and had no idea why she was being arrested. That footage was shared by fellow British athlete, and legend, Linford Christie. That footage went viral, becoming an international news story. Despite the Met's protestations that there were no concerns here with the officer's conduct, that wasn't what we found following our investigation.

Earlier that year, 32-year-old Dwayne Francis had too, found himself at the centre of an illegal stop and search by Met police. His crime? Waiting in his car for the post office to open so that he could carry out an errand before his working day at a local secondary school began.

Then came the case of Jordan Walker-Brown, a young Black man who was paralysed from the chest down following a taser deployment from a police officer as he jumped over a wall and landed sickeningly headfirst. Jordan was running away from police at the time.

And there was the case of Child Q. This was the case of a 15-year-old Black schoolgirl who was wrongly accused of having drugs and then strip-searched by Met officers with no appropriate adult present, while she was on her period. Even describing the circumstances of this investigation are shocking and this case provoked understandably considerable community anger and protests more widely. It was a horrendous case but from which I would use to challenge the Met and the way it approached strip-searching of children.

There were a series of events between the Met and Black communities that over those coming months, became very viral, very quickly. All causing huge tension between the Met and Black communities, when these very issues were of global interest. There are far too many to name each individually, but one case that I have to mention, and one that will always remain with me, is that of Nicole Smallman, and Biba Henry.

Even before we took on this independent investigation, I knew about it. Their murder was absolutely horrific, heartbreaking. Two young sisters doing exactly what they should be doing, celebrating a birthday with the people they loved, killed in the most barbaric way. The way their family was treated in the aftermath? Awful, but the family's grief was to be compounded.

Once the sisters had been found, (by family members who had been forced to conduct their own missing persons search), while guarding the crime scene, two Met police officers took selfies with their bodies, sharing the images in WhatsApp groups alongside the caption:

"Unfortunately I'm sat next to two dead birds full of stab wounds."

An anonymous tip-off brought this to light, and both individuals have since been jailed and barred from ever being able to serve with the police again. I won't waste anymore words on them, they aren't worth the paper. Instead, I'd like to pay my respect to Nicole and Bibba's mother, Reverend Mina Smallman. Since the murder of her daughters and the events that followed, Mina Smallman has campaigned tirelessly for much needed police reform. I've seen her take on Chief Constables firsthand, cutting through the corporate bullshit and calling it out for what it is.

She's just an amazing, inspirational human being, and policing would do well to genuinely listen to her.

In the face of evil, she demonstrated decency and light, and a level of courage that I still struggle to comprehend.

In amongst the cases I've just mentioned, you had all the *other* independent investigations, of which there are many. I honestly don't know where that year went. I fitted about five years' worth of experience into one, both in terms of case volume, and severity.

To their credit, in some ways, the Met did step up to the plate that summer. Following on from the murder of George Floyd, I remember one Met Commander setting up a forum. I remember it very well, and I should do, I was part of it. The group brought together serving officers and members of the community and was a safe space where people could openly talk about the issues taking place at that time, and the implications this had for minoritised Londoners. As you can imagine, it facilitated some *really* difficult conversations.

Footage would be shared within the group that showed members of the Black community in altercations with the police. Often, this footage would be something that had already gone viral, and as such was highly contentious. Often, unless there was a glaringly obvious case of misconduct that was overt and impossible to deny, the police wouldn't see an awful lot wrong with it.
Community members would watch the same footage and would share their concerns with what they were seeing.

And there it was, that literal gap in understanding.

Two polarised binary positions were established, despite viewing the same incident. There, encapsulated the very essence of why the Met struggled so much with maintaining the confidence of Black communities. They just didn't see what the problem was.

It shone a light on the *lack* of understanding that policing had on the experience of young Black people. It also shone a light on the fact that there are officers out there who want that to change.

As the person representing the independent regulator, my toes were held to the fire as well, many times. And I understood why. But the intention of the forum was good, and vital conversations were had. I was keen to support it. One theme that consistently came through was the use of stop and search against Black communities. It was the totemic issue.

I'm no stranger to the racial profiling that provides the basis for far too many a stop and search, having myself been subject to a vehicle stop more than once for no other reason than being a young, brown man behind the wheel of a flash car. Now, here I was, in a role where I could put that issue under the lens, with levers at my disposal to potentially drive some positive change in the area. I was keen to do this as authentically as possible, listening to those most affected and ensuring that their voice provided the foundations for the work, and its outcome alongside the evidence.

And that's exactly what we did.
Working with communities, and experts in the field, we used our evidence base to make 11

systemic recommendations to the Metropolitan Police Service. These recommendations looked at the fundamental flaws within their use of stop and search as a policing tactic, listing what needed to be done to reduce disproportionality and racial bias from its use in London. That was the first substantive work the IPCC/IOPC had done on stop and search in a decade. Those recommendations were about as hard hitting as they could be in the system I operated in.

I sent them to the Met in advance, as is general practice, alongside a briefing that clearly covered what was coming and how we'd got there. I was sure to make it clear that significant engagement had taken place to ensure the report was based on those most affected by the issues being discussed, and those with expertise in that specific area. We're talking Y-Stop; Stopwatch; the National Police Chief Council's national stop and search lead, the College of Policing, HMICFRS (the inspectorate), local Councilors and, most importantly; communities and young people.

The Met rejected every single recommendation.

I read the rejection letter and took a breath, uttering expletives that ended with a firm "for *fuck's* sake". I remember thinking," Surely, *this can't be right? How can they reject what's there in black and white?!"*

I couldn't take their rejection lying down, I just couldn't, and I wouldn't. So, I went to the Mayor's Office, to the Deputy Mayor of Policing and Crime. I said to them:

"Look, really? If this is their answer I'll go out and publish it, but you might want to have a look at this yourself."

Her office did. The Met came back, full of apologies for 'accidentally' rejecting all 11 recommendations. Accidentally.

We published them, and as part of the campaign to share the work nationally, I did a day of media with numerous outlets who could share what we had found, and what we were recommending, widely. Then, something strange happened.

The people that had initially been at the front of the queue to knock me and slate the work I was doing? They were saying really nice things. They were backing the work we'd done. They were backing me, even. They rated the way I'd done things, and the collaborative approach that I'd taken in putting it together which, for reasons that I'll never understand, I'd had to really fight for internally. I still remember one community elder say in a meeting in which the Met were present, after I had presented our work on these stop and search recommendations:

"I stand with Sal."

"I stand with the IOPC."

This *never* happened. And yet, here it just had.

If nothing else, it gave me the reassurance that to truly do the right thing sometimes you just have to block out the noise, trust your gut and keep moving forward. And I'm so glad I did.

That work led to me taking on responsibility for the IOPC Race Discrimination team, as the National Strategic Lead. This work looked to tackle racial discrimination not just in stop and search, but across policing as a whole. That included all manner of things, from use of force, to taser, to courtesy and respect, something so human, so basic, but *so* often lacking in conversations between police and communities.

At the time of its launch, it was described by the Guardian as one of '*the 20 most significant moments since the Macpherson enquiry, for Black and minority ethnic communities*'.

Honestly, that meant nothing to me. Doing something with the opportunity we had, however, meant everything. It felt like a generational moment, and there was a window of opportunity to do something and leverage the powers at my disposal to drive real, meaningful change.

I was the first person of colour in my role, and I was mindful to use that difference to do different things, in a way that made an impact. I was clear from the very beginning that in doing this work, engagement with those most affected was key. I was clear that I wanted to take an approach that centered around:

"This is what you told us; this is what we did."

Not talking *at* communities, which far too many organisations do. I called it the rhetoric trap, and I wasn't going to fall into it. It was a non-negotiable in taking the job and was the start of many fights.

My first fight was getting the green light to set up an Independent National Advisory Group. This group brought together key figures from the race discrimination arena to discuss the decades-old, and emerging issues being faced by communities. To me, these authentic voices were an essential component in helping to shape every output of that programme of work, with the best, most authentic insight. It was absolutely instrumental in the delivery of that work, just as I knew it would be.

Then came the fight to drive the stop and search work already undertaken in London, nationally. Stop and search is far from a Met-centric issue, and it was badly needed. I wasn't backing down on that one either, and we delivered a national report that recommended not only changes to policing practice, but changes to the law in how stop and search is conducted across England and Wales[39].

I knew that we had one shot at what we were doing and before long, publicly, I began to front it for the organisation. Comfort zone or not, it wasn't a time to sit quietly in the background. I wanted people to see and hear what we were

---

[39] National stop and search learning report | Independent Office for Police Conduct (IOPC)

doing. Not for an ego massage. God no. But to shine a light on the issues being faced by communities, and the work being done to reassert new 'norms' in societal, systemic behaviour. I was prepared to throw myself into the media circus if it meant those issues got the coverage they so badly needed.

My family saw what I was doing, and we had some really surreal experiences.

My first TV slot was on Channel 4 News and covered the officers being arrested for taking selfies at the murder scene of Reverend Smallman's daughters. They filmed the interview in advance, in what they call a pre-record. I watched it through gritted fingers, wincing and willing the slot to end so I could turn to my family for a full and honest debrief.

Shortly after, me and the kids were in the garden, me taking in the fresh air and processing the nerves that come from watching yourself get grilled by a journalist for the first time. We could hear our neighbour's TV blasting out the Channel 4 News theme tune and watching me. All a bit surreal. That was a moment when it really hit me how pivotal the media was in maintaining a national conversation on these issues.

We were midway through a heatwave and the BBC approached me, asking if I would film an interview as part of a documentary they were putting together, that looked at the disproportionate use of force in policing. It was *boiling*, that thick, humid heat that we just aren't equipped for in England. The production team came to the house, and given the temperature, began to set up in the back garden while I got suited and booted. The disproportionate use of force is nothing new in policing, it's something that has always been there unfortunately. But this was the summer of 2020, and that issue was firmly under the spotlight, and in the investigations that were coming into my team thick and fast. I could talk to that issue all day.

Just as we're getting to an intense part of the conversation, Darwin, my grumpy old tabby cat, decided to stretch his legs and attack the carefully placed cables, sending the whole thing into chaos. My eldest son had to come carry Darwin off stage left, as my family watched in hysterics fogging the patio doors in laughter. I regrouped with the crew and the conversation continued.

My kids heard me speak about things that might well have resonated with them:

- Racism
- Culture
- The need for change

They saw me transition from their dad, someone who was battling outside of his own comfort zone and working to find his voice, to someone who could confidently articulate themselves on the issues being discussed in front of a camera crew.

And it was them who made it possible.
They were, and still are, my rock.

I threw everything at it. I worked ridiculous hours, and it was hard. While leading on the issues on racial discrimination nationally, I had accountability for all of the cases coming in involving the Met. Alongside all of that, I was handling my own very real, very raw bereavement in the background, something that I was definitely compartmentalising.

I still think we could've done more.

We should have been on the likes of CNN, part of the conversation on the issues within US policing. But, I was one person, and like it or not there were ceilings around me and a limited number of hours in the day. I felt like a lone wolf in a lot of the work I did. I really wish I'd had that support, to get even more reach and impact than we did manage. But I also colluded with some really great, hardworking, and *passionate* people. We pushed hard to get into that difficult, contentious space. There are too many individual people to mention here, and they might just kill me for doing so, but you know who you are.

We're talking about 2020, four years ago now. But, what that year did for me I still feel today. It gave me a voice, and a national platform which I was privileged to have then and am privileged to have now. I still use that platform today to bring hidden issues to the forefront of conversation. It's part of the reason I'm writing this book. But, as I've alluded to already, it wasn't easy to get there. Like any tough time in life, you look back now and think how did I do it? But you do, don't you? Especially when the stakes are so high, and important. You do it remembering who you are, following your true north.

The IOPC had been given new powers, one of which was called the 'Power of Own Initiative'. Although they had been much touted, they hadn't been used. This power meant that the

IOPC could start an independent investigation without waiting for the force to send it in themselves, something that can take considerable time. If something met a certain criteria, and was serious enough, you could treat it as 'referred'. Once you'd done that, you could begin your independent investigation there and then, without delay.

I was the first person at the IOPC to use that power. Not once, not twice, but three times. I used it before we even had a proper process in place.

One weekend, footage began to circulate on social media of a Black woman, surrounded by five Met police officers and saying, "*I can't breathe.*" They had restrained her on the ground and there were questions to be asked about the proportionality of the level of force used by the officers. She was lying on her front, being restrained, with the officers pinning her down, The imagery here, at that time, was incredibly emotive. I viewed the footage, I trusted my gut, and I used this new power. I found out afterwards that the Met were pissed off. A Met Commander asked me quite bluntly:

"Why didn't you call me first? Why didn't you just ask me?"

I was equally as blunt:
"I did. I tried to call you; you didn't pick up."

When things like that happen, you have to step up, and make the decision that best aligns with you, your values, and your role, whatever that might be. You have to make the call, and that was the right call.

Another case that came in featured the father of rapper Wretch 32, and the inappropriate use of force. The Met were dragging their heels in sending it to us to review, and frankly, having seen the footage I wasn't willing to accept this. The footage showed an officer from the Met using their taser on an elderly Black man inside his home who consequently fell down his stairs. The Met refused to refer this to the IOPC. So, I used this power again. It set a marker. If you are not going to send these things in, I will use the powers at my disposal. Tough shit if that upsets you, that's not my lookout. Human beings are human beings and, typically, if you give some people an inch they'll take a mile. So don't give that inch. Without fear or favour was the most important call to action for me in my role, and in quite a puritan way, it was how I conducted it.

The Met were pissed off and briefed against me/the IOPC to the Home Office about how I/the IOPC was using this new power indiscriminately. I wasn't, but this was how the Met operated. And sure enough, I then got that insipid limp hand on my shoulder from someone senior. I was very comfortable with my decisions, but now there was a sudden urgency to develop guidance on these new powers. Fine, that actually would have been helpful if I'd had that at the time. Subsequently this new guidance was based on my emails and centered around how I exercised my decision-making.

Interestingly, what my approach did here was set new boundaries with the Met. Whereas previously they would resist referring setting matters to us to consider whether we should investigate, now the conversation would be:

Met: *If we don't send this will you use your new Power?*
Me: *Yep.*
Met: *Ok, we'll send it in.*

Progress, of sorts.

It was a year of fighting. Fighting to do things the way I felt was necessary. But winning all those bruising fights gave me so much confidence in myself, and my judgment.

Looking back now, I should have looked after myself a bit better, but I'd take back nothing professionally.

I wouldn't change a thing.

Chapter 8
Having my day in court

Idiom: to have your day in court
Definition: to get an opportunity to give
your opinion on something or to explain
your actions after they have been criticised.

You could argue that this book in its entirety is me having my day in court, on paper and in black and white. At the time of writing this book, however, I'd just had my actual day in court, on the stand, and in front of the very person who had put me there.

It was a day that had been hanging over me for four years, and all because of a decision that I had been required to make, as part of my job.

That decision led to me being treated in a way that, for me, speaks *massively* to the treatment of senior leaders of colour in our society today. It linked directly to a case that I mentioned earlier and involved the stop and search of Bianca Williams and Ricardo Dos Santos, arguably the most high-profile stop and search of the last decade.

It wasn't the case itself that had led me to the courtroom. I was standing in the midst of an employment tribunal, an employment tribunal that was centred around the ego of a disgruntled former "colleague". This individual had been an Investigator at the IOPC.

For the purpose of this chapter, I was tempted to call her many things, but it's probably best to refer to her just as *the LI (Lead Investigator).*

After taking the job as Regional Director, I'd been met with heavy scepticism from some from the moment I set foot in the role. Here I was, this South-Asian bloke with a thick Scottish accent, fresh from the Assessment Unit and living in Birmingham, way outside the M25 circular.

I'd been the rank outsider to get the job. I was the outsider of outsiders. And yet I'd got it, but it became clear fairly quickly that me gaining the position had really pissed *some* people off.

The case of Williams and Dos Santos was already high profile. Here we had two well-respected athletes, who had been subjected to a vehicle stop and then a stop and search under the premise that drugs and/or weapons may be in the car. Footage of the stop went viral on social media because it had been shared by Linford Christie OBE, British athlete, and legend. A headline at the time read:

Linford Christie furiously accuses the Met of institutional racism after two Black athletes are stopped, manhandled from their car outside their home and searched in London - but Scotland Yard claims they 'sped off'.

The footage was a hard watch, with Bianca Wiliams visibly upset, telling officers that her young child was in the car. At the time of this incident, her son was three months old.

Tensions around the legality of the stop were simmering, remember this was when the issues around trust and confidence between the Met and Black communities was in the sharpest of media glares for the past decade in the summer of 2020. Then, on 22nd July 2020, Cressida Dick (the Met Commissioner at the time) went onto the radio and decided to say that having viewed the footage themselves, the Met didn't actually believe that there was anything particularly wrong with what had taken place that day.

This was *hugely* controversial and an outrageous statement for the Commissioner to have made with an independent investigation ongoing to determine this very point. This was the Met's incalculable arrogance on full display, and their disdain for the IOPC didn't really need to be inferred.

I knew from that moment onwards that any decision we made would be *heavily* scrutinised.

Because of the Commissioner's statement, I had to get more involved in this investigation.

One of my Operations Managers was the decision-maker but, because this had now become an international news story, it was right that I took on that role. After discussing this with him, we both agreed that was the right thing to do.

IOPC independent investigations exist in a niche world of regulatory jargon, process, and bureaucracy. One of these processes was that at the start of an investigation the appointed Lead Investigator would make what was called the initial severity assessment. Based on the available evidence is there an indication of misconduct or gross misconduct? In the vast majority of cases, they would make this initial decision assessment. Any final decision would then be handed over to a final decision-maker who would have access to the full investigation, all of the evidence, and make a decision on whether there was a case to answer for misconduct, or gross misconduct.

If yes to either, it's then sent back to the force for them to take forward any misconduct meeting or gross misconduct hearing through an independent misconduct panel.

That's the simplified version of the process.

I did say that's what would normally happen, but this wasn't a normal stop and search investigation. The Commissioner of the Metropolitan Police, the most senior officer in the country, had effectively said there was nothing to see here.

Given the significant risks associated with the investigation, I decided that it wasn't actually fair to put that sort of pressure onto a person at the grade of Lead Investigator to make that initial severity assessment. The pressure around it was palpable, and frankly *I* was being paid the sort of money that is aligned with that sort of decision and risk.

So, in this investigation I elevated this decision to myself, and our rules permitted this for unusual scenarios like this. This was communicated to the team by a colleague, and at that stage, no concerns were raised.

That weekend, which I remember clearly being a Bank Holiday weekend, I took home everything we had so far. I looked through the material that had been put together, and internally it became clear to me that I'd made the right call. The work I had in front of me could in no way withstand any level of scrutiny, or criticism. I reviewed the risk severity assessment and could see that having viewed the evidence, LI had come to the following conclusion: Gross Misconduct, for seven officers.

I looked at the evidence in front of me and could see that the rationale was massively flawed. Unlike the Met I *was* concerned about the actions of the officers, but Gross MIsconduct? At

244

that stage, I couldn't make that argument based on the evidence in front of me. For six of those officers, at that point I *could* argue a case to answer for Misconduct, confidently.

Even when I was writing up my rationale, I knew this would be contentious, and after a Bank Holiday weekend which passed me by as I spent it squinting at my laptop, I went back to work on Monday ready to update the team.

While I had expected my decision to be contentious, what I hadn't anticipated was that this would lead to an internal and then public smear campaign against me. A campaign that would land me in court four years later.

From the moment my update hit the inbox of the LI in question, I was public enemy number one.

She was determined to bring me down. Her own manager actually came to me and said:

"Sal you need to watch out. She quite clearly wants to go out with a bang."

In the coming weeks, news of this dissatisfaction became common knowledge within the office and wider organisation, with no attempt made to act with any sense of professionalism. These rumblings, and the potential impact they could have on a highly contentious investigation, made it clear that it wasn't suitable for the Lead Investigator to be a part of this investigation any longer. There were also some welfare issues that needed to be considered and handled with care and sensitivity.

But before any formal decision was made, they withdrew themselves from the investigation and, internally, the work continued. While it did, the LI in question continued on a campaign of "righteous" indignation. I was bad-mouthed to anyone who would listen, and those that did the bad-mouthing were largely those toxic disaffected individuals that stymie up lots of good organisations. Sadly, I was to learn my team had too many of them.

Externally, the change in Lead Investigator became an area of serious contention. Questions arose and given the nature of the work I was involved in, the risk appetite diminished.

My "manager" at the time decided that a peer review of my decision (to change investigator) should take place. This was a decision that I had already communicated to the Met, and a decision that had been ratified by a Senior Lawyer in true belt and braces fashion. This peer-review was hugely undermining, and it wasn't normal practice. In fact, I'd never heard of it before. What made it a particularly bitter pill to swallow was I later discovered that the review had only taken place to pacify the LI.

My decision-making was "ratified" by the peer-review and, as the ink dried on that decision, I discovered a grievance was being brought against me by the LI.

The *working hypothesis* was that I was corrupt and working to protect Cressida Dick. I use the words '*working hypothesis*' quite deliberately as this is a phrase the LI would cling onto as a shield of faux legitimacy in the absence of any evidence. The grievance process was then conducted in a way that was akin to an inquisition. Not in the way I was interviewed, but in the way a range of random people who had literally nothing to do with the investigation were interviewed and asked to give their view on '*what they thought of Sal*'.

While this grievance was rumbling on in the background, I was forwarded on an email where one of the disaffected had said some terrible stuff about me, really offensive things. I wasn't meant to see it of course, and I didn't share the fact that someone had shown me it in confidence. The chain was full of other colleagues, all of whom could see the things being said about me. The thing that actually stung was that no one had my back in the email chain, no one called this out. These remarks were offensive enough to warrant a disciplinary investigation in themselves, but of course that didn't happen. People didn't necessarily agree with what was being said, don't get me wrong. But no one stood up and called it out. And we were supposed to be a values-driven organisation.

Meanwhile, the grievance against me continued. It wasn't upheld and of course, was swiftly followed by an appeal. That too came to nothing. Just when I thought the process had been exhausted I found that a whistleblowing complaint had gone in. This time? It was about me and the Director General at the time, this time saying we were *both* corrupt.

(Sighs).

While I'm getting hammered internally, I'm getting a kicking externally too from the media.

While the whistleblowing complaint went on, so did work on the investigation. It was still high risk, it was painstaking work, and it was *very* high pressure. The Guardian then ran an article in which they hinted that the complainants within the case were set to withdraw. The journalist cited a lack of trust in the process, highlighting again the fact that the investigating team had changed.

I was giving everything I had to the investigation at the time, and articles like this one added fuel to an ever-growing fire,

I was too busy in the middle of the storm to do much about it, about my reputation. I was just trying to do the right thing by the role I was charged with, and to be led by the evidence and make sure we conducted the best possible investigation without fear or favour.

And so, I kept my head down, kept working, and didn't defend myself *at all*. I was focused on getting to the finish line, and the deafening noise around me wasn't going to stop me.

As the investigation progressed, we gained new insight and new evidence. One of the things I was determined to look at was this issue of racial bias within a police misconduct setting. Evidencing this has been a systemic issue in misconduct settings, but in a case like this, the issue of bias was critical in the absence of any overt racism. That was a line of enquiry I ensured was followed robustly, although incredibly difficult. After a period, the evidential picture had changed enough for me to reassess the initial severity assessments. In doing so I determined that now there was an indication that five officers met the threshold for Gross Misconduct, with one other officer remaining at Misconduct, as before.

In the background, the whistleblowing investigation continued until in February 2022, it concluded, and it came to nothing.

Why?

Because I'm not corrupt.

I'd been off sick for a period of time before that, which had nothing to do with any of that nonsense. The reasons behind that I'll go into later.

I came back to work, and the LI who had been trying with every process in the system to get rid of me, had resigned. From what I was told, it was because they hadn't liked the outcome of that whistleblowing exercise. They'd even tried to launch a complaint into the whistleblowing process, saying that it was inadequate. But when that was rejected, I can only assume that they'd run out of options.

I brushed myself off and went back to the investigation that I was dealing with, fighting the Met at every corner. It was relentless and all the way through this investigation the Met resisted the very notion that there was *any* misconduct present in the actions of any of these officers.

Then, something interested happened when I communicated my final decision to the Met that I believed there was a case to answer for the following:

Five officers: Gross Misconduct
One officer: Misconduct

Among many things for two of the officers I determined they had a case to answer for breaching the professional standard relating to honesty and integrity, as I believed the evidence showed they were lying when they said one of the complainants smelt of cannabis. I also believed five of the officers had a case to answer for breaching equality & diversity as there was evidence of racial bias. There was much more and if you have a spare evening, you can read the 222-page report on the IOPC website[40].

After two years of maintaining that there was nothing to see here, the Met changed their position overnight and agreed with me that two of the officers did have a case to answer for Gross Misconduct (for lying) but not the others. I directed the Met to hold a Gross Misconduct Hearing for all five officers, as I had the power to do.

At this point, despite the challenges with this investigation, I'd actually managed to engage the two complainants, Bianca and Ricardo, alongside specialist counsel who helped us to look into the difficult area of racial bias in a

---

[40] Ms Bianca Williams and Mr Ricardo Dos Santos investigation report | Independent Office for Police Conduct (IOPC)

police misconduct setting. Counsel agreed with my decision-making that there was evidence present to support racial bias. The decisions I had made here hadn't been made before and would now be tested in the independent police misconduct panel that would be held.

In February 2022 I'd just delivered the Operation Hotton Report, the investigation that lifted the lid on Charing Cross Police station, a cesspit of misogyny, racism, every ism you can think of. But coming out of what had been a global news story I didn't really get a chance to catch my breath before I found that the LI was now looking to go public with her *working hypothesis*. They'd approached a journalist and the BBC who, having heard her story, had confirmed they were going to run with it.

But that wasn't the worst part. Not really.

The worst part for me was I had no right of reply. Not unless I wanted to jeopardise the entire investigation, and potentially prejudice the pending Gross Misconduct hearing. And that was totally non-negotiable. If nothing else, it would have been an immoral thing to do to the complainants, who had been through so much already. So, I had to put my own fight, and my own pride back into a box and lock it up. The LI evidently didn't give a shit about potentially jeapordising any of the above. It was all about the spotlight.

The BBC ran with that story *all* day. Trailing it and advertising the Newsnight investigation that was set to air that night.

Despite having the slight benefit of being warned, throughout the day my name (and that of the Director General) was dragged through the mud. My mind was spinning with thoughts of what the evening's broadcast might bring. I didn't have anything to hide, but why let the truth get in the way of a good story?

That day I was in London, in a really busy office that sits in the heart of Canary Wharf. Here I was in the headquarters of an organisation with people all around me, and yet I had never felt more alone.

Two people came up to me and asked how I was, to check that I was okay, and I'll remember their kindness. But everyone else ignored me. These weren't my people. I don't know why I expected anything different, my own moment of weakness, I think. I sat in that open-plan office silenced, while the media circus around me carried on. Thing is, I'm not built to sit on my hands, I've fought my whole life. But here I had to sit there and just take it, getting punched in the face. I was being vilified but I had no voice, no corporate line, no nothing. I couldn't help but think:

"These fucking bastards."
I just wanted to come home.

By the time I stepped through the front door it was late and I was feeling pretty sorry for myself. Just done *in* by the whole day and by the months that had led up to it. I braced myself for the show and sat down with my family to watch it. We watched, waiting for some substance, some evidence, just *something.* I couldn't believe the LI actually used the phrase '*my working hypothesis'* admitting there was no actual evidence for any of this. The discussion then went into the studio between the lead journalist and Kirsty Wark, but there was no knockout blow. It just kind of meandered into a cul-de-sac and stopped.

My wife turned to me:

"Is that it?"

The next day the text messages came pinging, reassuring me that it had been a bunch of nonsense. But that wasn't the end of it, next came a crime reporter. In a two-page splash, chunks were torn out of me, trashing other staff from the IOPC in the process. That didn't get much coverage to be honest, I think any credibility in the LI was somewhat lacking at that point. It still grated though, to know that lies were being printed about me, there for anyone to read.

It's easy to say, it doesn't matter. But when you haven't done anything wrong, and you have to suffer an injustice, it's difficult to just sit with it.

It was a horrible time, and for what?

To me, this wasn't about the decision I had made, although it had been dressed up as being *all* about that. At the heart of this was a bruised ego, an ego that couldn't quite believe that I, this South-Asian man who says Aye and not yes, had questioned a decision.

Because who the fuck was *I*, to do *that*?

And it wasn't finished yet.

Enter stage left, the employment tribunal.

At this point, I'd left the IOPC. Legally however, I was still obliged to appear at the tribunal. In fairness to the IOPC, they wanted to defend the nonsense claims being made. It was a time that I'd put to the back of my mind, as you do when something shitty happens to you. But, as the tribunal loomed, I knew I'd have to reopen that box and get myself up to speed with everything that had happened, to present my own experience in as thorough a way as possible.

In the run up, I'd been sent the bundle of evidence, which is standard practice in that situation. I wanted to prepare myself properly, and so over a weekend I'd sat down to read through it, taking my mind back to that time so that I, and my memory, was fresh. I didn't realise just *how* bad it had been until I did that, until I'd reflected on the two and a half thousand pages that lay in front of me. I didn't actually expect to feel the way I did, but in reading through what were effectively my memories in print, I actually felt sorry for myself back then because I didn't have a clue. I looked at it through the lens of hindsight and realised there were five or six people actively trying to get rid of me. I came across an email chain which recorded the LI saying:

"*I'm going to get rid of him. I'm going to go out with a bang.*"

It was triggering because I hadn't realised just how awful they had been at the time. Professionally, I'd been too busy working on high-profile investigations, batting off the media and dealing with the deluge of cases that were coming in from every angle. I was right in the middle of it all. Personally? At that time, I was already nearly at breaking point, or maybe *at* breaking point. And amongst all of that, here were supposed colleagues orchestrating a full-throated witch hunt against me, outsider, because who the *fuck* was *he* to make that decision*, who the fuck was he* to know better than a *lead investigator*? The decision I made was based entirely on the evidence and within my gift as a decision-maker.

This individual did not get their way in the workplace. So they cried (literally), got attention and then complained, and when things still didn't go their way? They stamped their feet and complained that bit louder. And the organisational, system response was to essentially put an arm round them and be seen to cater to every demand. Me, a *brown* man, and the most senior leader of colour *in* the organisation at the time, who at no point did anything wrong, was then put through the meat grinder to appease. Zero organisational thought was given to my welfare.

There was not a *shred* of actual evidence to justify any of that bullshit. When I look back, I should have had a thought for myself, and how I was being treated, but I just took it. I can't turn back the clock, but I keep thinking about it now. I was one of the most senior people of colour in that entire system, I was out there talking about systemic race discrimination but look at the reality of my treatment by my own organisation.

When you boil it down, you can see things a bit more clearly. You can see the disproportionate criticism, you can see the different standards you're being held to, and you can see that systemic indifference. When you look and reflect on these experiences you can start to understand just why *so* many ethnic minorities end up only being that tiny number at a senior level, and when they do how they can end up standing in the corner shouting into the dark:

"This is racism, this is what racial bias looks like."

This insidious, gaseous, gaslighting entity that you can never quite pin down.

When you tally these things up, what happened to me by any objective measure was at its best unfair and at it its worst tells the story of what racial bias can look like in the workplace. Even in an independent regulator. It was only on reading through the evidence bundle that I realised this. It was an audit trail and proof of the witch-hunt I felt was happening at the time but couldn't see fully. A witch-hunt enabled by the organisational system response throughout.

The biggest irony here was that the people who professed to be standing up for the rights of Black complainants were persecuting me, a person of colour - and truly didn't care about that.

I read that evidence once, and that was enough.

It was four days before the employment tribunal was set to take place.

I'd met the barrister before; I'd met the solicitor, and we'd had a case conference to cover the essentials. I was the "star" witness for the IOPC because when you *really* get down to it, at the centre of this tribunal was the LI's vendetta against me. I say that confidently because, having seen the evidence bundle and the way the case was set to be shaped, a lot of it revolved around me and my decision making. This was something that had nothing to do with any dismissal necessarily, in a tribunal that was taking place to deal with an allegation of constructive dismissal. Nevertheless, I knew that four years later, I'd be on the stand, examined by counsel under oath, as to why *I* did what *I* did.

Work, as ever, was incredibly busy in the lead up. I busied myself during the day with that, and in the evenings, I set about preparing myself for what was to come.
Before I knew it, it was the morning of the tribunal itself.

That morning was spent on autopilot. I'd woken up at 4am, got myself ready and headed towards the train station to catch the train into London. My start to the day had been one of deliberate solitude. I'd had to stop my wife and eldest daughter from coming with me. Despite them being desperate to come down in support, I told them:

"It would actually be easier for me, if you didn't."

I did that not to be a martyr, but because I had no idea how the day would pan out, what would be said, and how it would affect me. I guess in some way, I wanted to protect them from the onslaught that I might be walking into.

Hurtling along the tracks, I read over my witness statement, and then I stopped, putting it back into my bag where it would stay for the rest of the day. When I got into London, I took the well-trodden path to the Underground and boarded the Jubilee Line. Normally, whenever I'm on the tube I wear Air Pods, but on that day I didn't. I wanted to be alone with my thoughts and God. I asked:

"Let me represent myself to the best of my ability."

All I planned to do was tell the truth. That was the single line in my strategy. I had zero to hide, and in truth *Inshallah* would be my guide. I would tell them what I did, why I did it, and answer any questions they had about what had happened, because that is what *had* happened. My truth would be my true north throughout the conversation.

I arrived in East London and wandered around squinting at Google maps on my phone until I eventually found it. I had walked past it a couple of times. It was a lovely development straight off India Docks. There were ponds, bridges, and little independent cafes dotted about, playing music that travelled from the warm inside to the cold outdoors. Surrounded by these lovely buildings and taking it all in, a big red dot on my phone told me I'd arrived at my destination. *"This can't be it."*

So I walked around some more, hoping for a reroute, but it kept bringing me back. It was quite a surreal setting, especially given the day that lay ahead. I'd expected an ancient sandstone building, the musty scent hitting you as you enter. I thought I might bump into the complainant down a dimly lit, mottled corridor. But there was none of that. It turned out that this tribunal had one floor in this quite swanky, floor-to-ceiling glass building. I made a note mentally that one day, I should bring my wife there. And then I went in.

The security was ridiculous with scanners for just about *everything*. I even had to sip my water, to prove it was nothing dodgy. That was new. There was a separate entrance for the complainant, which I thought was a good idea. The whole set up was decidedly thorough. I met with the barrister, and we went up together. She was really lovely, and as I was about to find out utterly formidable in the courtroom.

The further in that we got, the clearer it became that yes, we were indeed inside a Government building. Beige walls, tatty chairs, and a round wooden table that was adorned with nothing but coffee rings on the veneered beech surface. There were no refreshments, put it that way.

We sat down and spoke about the evidence bundle that she too had obviously seen. I spoke to her about the fact that this day marked the end of four difficult years for me, in which I'd effectively been gagged and unable to defend myself. I won't speak on behalf of the barrister because that isn't fair. But it *is* fair to say that she understood quite clearly what I'd been through.

An IOPC representative was there with us to provide support from a welfare perspective, but

I'd really needed that welfare four years earlier not now. But it was a nice gesture. In conversation I did say pointedly:

"Have you read that evidence?"

They hadn't, which was fine. But given their role in HR, I continued:

"When you have a particularly boring Sunday afternoon, have a look at it and see how I was treated, because I'll tell you now it wasn't good. Someone else would have broken."

They just did that thing, when people look intently but don't do or say anything to indicate any form of agreement.

The barrister and I then went over the layout of the courtroom, and despite being less formal than the courts you see on the TV (given that it was an employment tribunal), it still is a court. It still had judges, a legal team, a witness in the stand, etc etc. The good part is, you got to sit down, and so we sat down, ready.

In front of me were eight lever-arch files that contained the two and half thousand pages of evidence. I knew already how this would play

out. I would be asked a question, I'd have to find the folder, find the piece of evidence in question, and then respond. I had folders across the desk, folders at my feet and they were *huge*.
I prepared myself mentally for navigating these and continued to sit.
Waiting.

At the far end of the room was a wooden raised level that the judges would sit behind throughout the day. Closest to me was a row of tables where the barristers would sit and the LI, who sat within my eyeline. Then, you had a public gallery section behind this row of tables. There were a couple of members of staff from the IOPC HR team, and a couple more who I expect, were there on behalf of the 'other side'. There was also a big TV on the stand with someone attending on Zoom, who I assume was most likely the journalist the LI had gone to.
The judge came in, flanked by two panel members. One man, and two women.

"All rise."

We all rose.

"Please be seated."

This up and down happened throughout the day, as panel members came in, came out, and as the court room retired. It all felt surreal, the official nature of the whole thing played out in real life and not the telly. The only thing that differed from the courtrooms you do see on TV was the fact that you don't call the judge 'your honour'. In an employment tribunal you just call them 'Judge', or 'Sir/Madam'.

Throughout the day, I could feel the LI looking at me. I didn't catch eye contact at all, but I could *feel* it, in the way you *can* feel when someone is watching you. It didn't actually bother me, which was strange. I think it's because the whole thing very much felt like an out of body experience. Throughout my life, I've had to fight for a lot of things, and admittedly I have a hot temper. But I checked in with myself, and decided internally that, "No, I'm not here to be bitter or settle scores." No one was going to get a rise out of me emotionally, my composure would be my power.

I was there to tell the truth. That was it.

For the next four hours I settled into the swing of things, getting used to the setting and the way in which things worked in a tribunal of its kind. No one can really prepare you for that, it was a case of going through the motions, in real time. I answered the questions that were posed and answered them factually.

The reality is that opposing counsel are there to trip you up. They have to cherry pick the pieces of evidence that support their argument, and question you in a way that hopefully, makes you contradict yourself. Firing questions at me, they had me jumping from folder to folder:

"Pick up file 3, page 726, sub section 4. What do you think of this Mr Naseem?"

Onto the next folder.

"File 7, page 968, sub section 2.

Well Mr Naseem, what do you think of this? What do you think of that, Mr Naseem?"

But I'd done my homework and very quickly, I got into the rhythm.

This dance turned into a boxing match, and somehow, I don't know *how* exactly, that barrister was not able to lay a glove on me. There was one time where she *nearly* did, but it was at a time where she had introduced something that she shouldn't have. My barrister intervened and had it thrown out, which was without argument.

As well as being factual, at times I would pointedly say when things had been ridiculous. I really used my voice. I'd refer myself to the folder where emails had been exchanged that totally tore apart the argument being put in front of me. I'd do it in a way that showed no emotion, but in a way that was calm, measured, and based *entirely* on the evidence.

At one stage, they put forward the premise that somehow, Cressida Dick was linked to the criminal investigation around Michael Lockwood, the former Director General of the IOPC. It was big news at the time, and it was a cheap shot. They alluded to the fact that the decision I'd made years prior, was somehow to do Cressida Dick a favour, a '*you scratch our back we'll scratch yours*', type thing. To be clear, I'd known nothing of the charges relating to Michael Lockwood at the time I'd made the decision and, that aside, the Met had absolutely nothing to do with it, it was Humberside police that investigated this. It was ridiculous all round, but the judge allowed the question:

"Were you aware of the investigation surrounding Michael Lockwood?"

I told them I was not.

The judge then looked disapprovingly at the opposing counsel:

"Alright, what's next?"

When they started to go down the corruption road again, this time the judge *wouldn't* allow the question. Like I said earlier, opposing counsel will try to trip you up in any way they can. It got to the point that I was being asked for an opinion on why people might have said what they'd said. It was clutching at straws at best. Who the hell knows why people say the things they do? You tell me. Add to this that *some* of the people mentioned hadn't actually been involved in the investigation, they'd got their insight from the internet.

I mean, come on.

The opposing counsel then started to question my credentials, the inference being because I wasn't a Lead Investigator I wasn't qualified to make the decisions that I did.

I knew that thanks to the first grievance process
the LI started to bring my credentials into
question and made it quite clear that they had
concerns on whether or not I was up to the job.
I'm not the sort of person to slap my credentials
on the table, but in this courtroom it was the time
to do this. So, I pointed out that only one of us
has had a law degree. Only *one* of us went to
the best law schools in Scotland. Only *one* of us
has been a decision maker at three different
regulatory bodies, where decisions I made have
all been potentially challengeable by judicial
review, to a number in the thousands. I was paid
to be a decision-maker, not a Lead Investigator,
and that's exactly the skill set and experience I
brought to bear in the matter. I took my
satisfaction from the slight shuffle of discomfort
from the LI in their seat.

The boxing match continued, and I batted off
question after question about what I thought of
this, and what I thought of that. I then got asked:

*"Do you agree that it can't be wrong that
numerous witnesses have come to the
conclusion together that you, Mr Naseem, are
corrupt?"*

I remember quite pointedly saying:

"I can agree that it's a lot of nonsense."

My barrister would later tell me that it was in the top 20 lines she'd heard in a courtroom, not necessarily in *what* I'd said, but in the delivery. It completely decimated their argument for the joke that it was, with those in the public gallery stifling their laughter in the aftermath, I later discovered.

I'd make my point, counsel would have nothing to come back with, and onto the next question. That was pretty much the rhythm for the rest of the day.

Then it was time for the tribunal to ask questions.

The judge asked me a question, as did a member of the panel. They asked me if on reflection, I'd have done things differently. I did reflect, and the one thing I would have changed was the way I'd communicated my decision to the team. I'd been completely immersed in another investigation at the time and so had delegated that role to a senior member of my team, only speaking directly to the team in the weeks after. It was by no means done with intentional malice or disregard.

Then, it was time for my final cross examination by my barrister. The first question was just a yes or no answer, and then she asked me an open question about my time at the IOPC, a question framed in a way that allowed me to tell the tribunal who I was. She gave me a gift that I will always be thankful for.

I'd prepared absolutely nothing, but ended up giving a closing statement that was clearly influenced by all of the courtroom dramas I had watched.

I spoke about why I had taken the job, about my values, and about how I believed in doing the job without fear or favour. I talked to Op Hotton, and the decision I made to publish the messages and the *consequences* of that decision. The Mayor at the time getting involved as a direct result, the resignation of Cressida Dick, the very woman I was accused of supporting.

I spoke about what it was like for me in that position, the surreal statement that I was one of the most senior people of colour in that system at the time, and what that looked like in reality. The disproportionate criticism, being held to a different standard entirely, the blinding public glare on *everything* that I did.

I spoke to the *personal* impact of the past four years. How I'd had to sit on my hands with no right to reply, while my name was trashed publicly with lie after lie. I spoke to the impact that it had on my family, which is something I'm still very sore about. Why should they have had to watch their dad suffer? Why should they have had to endure that?

I spoke to what had happened to me at that organisation and called it out for what it was, a witch-hunt.

I asked the courtroom directly:

"Having outlined my experience can I ask what questions does that raise around racial bias and my treatment here? When all I did was try to do the right thing? When all I did was, my job?"

I was a bit emotional at the end. I'd spoken from the heart for a good five minutes after four years of silence. Allah gave me the ability to express myself that day to the *best* of my ability, just as I had asked. As a youngster, I'd been this scared wee boy with a stutter, who would freeze at just the thought of speaking publicly. But look what I'd done today. Me, an amateur, had outboxed a professional opponent.

To have on record my testimony, in an official setting, in front of the person who had orchestrated this witch-hunt against me, *who had bullied and harassed me*, was an enormous moment of catharsis. It was my last word, and the LI was watching me the whole time. This time, *they'd* had to stay silent.

Not many people get to do that, to express an injustice like that in the way that I was able to. I'll be forever thankful for that.

As I finished speaking, to my surprise one member of the panel was visibly emotional and glassy eyed. What I had said came unrehearsed, from the heart, but it must have resonated in a way that I hadn't fully understood. I was dismissed from my oath, and I left the courtroom. As I did, a couple of people whispered *"well done"* in hushed, well-meant support. Me and my barrister then went into a private room, where I immediately went to apologise.

"I shouldn't have said so much, I'm sorry."

Her only reply was to tell me that I'm one of the best witnesses she'd ever had.

We broke for lunch, and I spent the next hour in a total blur. I *do* remember ringing my wife the minute I left the building, to tell her what an incredible experience it had been. I remember telling her how Allah had helped me, not just in how to navigate the situation, but to give me that moment when I got to speak my truth in court. I was pretty euphoric, to be honest, my wife relieved in equal measure.

I was watching the landscape change as the train pulled out of Euston, staring absently out of the window watching, but not looking, and slowly realising something.

I was upset.

For four years I hadn't been upset. When it was happening to me I wasn't upset, but now that it was over? For some reason, I was, and I couldn't immediately understand why. In these past few years I'd blocked it all out and just taken it, and taken it, and taken it. They'd come at me, and they'd pummeled me, absolutely pummeled me. While it was going on, I hadn't *allowed* myself to get upset, why would I allow her and them to do that? I'd refused. Now, here I was, having to finally process all of that.

I got back, and of course the kids and my wife wanted to know *everything*. I told my wife how I was feeling.

The next day my wife had arranged for us to go out for breakfast and as I decompressed with her it dawned on me, why wouldn't I be? It was the first time in four years that I'd let my guard down, knowing that now there was an end to the punches and that finally, I'd put *my* truth out there.

The day after? I was good, after some much needed tlc from my wife.

All of this experience was meant for me.

I mean, not many people can say they made the main story of Newsnight, even though it was a load of bollocks.

I saw something the other day that resonated with me. It outlined two schools of thought:

- The system is broken and needs to be fixed.
- The system is working exactly as intended and needs to be destroyed.

White people have used systems to oppress people of colour since time began. This isn't just some working hypothesis that I've plucked from thin air, it's an age-old issue that has blighted those from marginalised backgrounds for centuries. I can't prove it, but I just don't think what I went through here would have reached that point in the first place, had I been White. I just don't. I don't believe that what happened to me would have happened at that level, and to that extent, if I didn't have this level of melanin in my skin.

And what a thing that is to say.

I *worked* in that system. But the system response reminded me in a very visceral, personal way to the concept that is institutional racism, and sometimes that you have to experience yourself to fully understand. And that can sometimes mean a collection of good people acting in unison unwittingly can still lead to this net result. It's an unexpected realisation from my time in the system and one I now only make with a bit of distance and time to reflect.

There is a residual anger left in me at what the system does, even when you try to do the right thing. How many other people get chewed up by the system for trying to do the right thing? How many *don't* make it out the other side? How many people *don't* get the chance to have their day in court, and the closure that brings?

When I left the court room, I didn't know the result of that tribunal was, and I didn't care.

To me, I was on trial that day, I'd been on trial for four years, and I won.

The case in question that led to me making the decision that I did, led to two officers being found guilty of Gross Misconduct. The Misconduct Panel initially found they had lied about the smell of cannabis being justification for the stop and lost their jobs as a result. That was off the back of the work my team did, the decision I made, and the bravery of the complainants who raised this. Bianca and Ricardo. Two young people who had done nothing wrong.
Once it became public news that the officers had been found guilty and subsequently struck off, a funding page set up. It was set up in support of these officers who at the time had been found guilty of Gross Misconduct and sacked. This appeal raised over £150,000. The Black victims were vilified, and the then two guilty White officers were rewarded. Even after the guilty

verdict at that time evidenced who was in the right, and the wrong.

These officers then appealed against their guilty verdicts and in October 2024 they won, overturning the Panel's original decision.

The reaction to the complainants? They were trolled and harassed on social media relentlessly.

Again.

This verdict is one that I've found to be deeply depressing given all of the evidence that I viewed. I know the ultimate decision was never one that was in my control but what this verdict does now show is the total incapability of the police complaints system to effectively deal with, or even understand, the legitimate concerns of Black communities in London in how stop and search is used against them.
It seems that in all of the vitriol which followed this verdict, the experience of Bianca and Ricardo didn't mention a second thought.

"What racialised stop and search is about, in London at least, is letting young black boys and men know their place in British society, letting them know who holds the power and showing them that their day can be held up even in a nice 'liberal' area like Camden in a way that will never happen to their White friends, if they still have any left by the time they have their first encounter with the police. It is about social engineering and about the conditioning of expectations, about getting black people used to the fact that they are not real and full citizens, so they should learn to not expect the privileges that would usually accrue from such a status. Racialised stop and search is also a legacy of more direct and brutal forms of policing the black body in the UK, from back in the days before political correctness."

Akala, Natives: Race and Class in the Ruins of Empire

Chapter 9
Marmite

"I've learned that people will forget what you said, people will forget what you did, but people will never forget how you made them feel."

Maya Angelou

My glasses keep fogging up.

I'm wearing one of those hospital issue face masks, the paper ones which were mandatory during peak Covid but for some time after, were still mandatory in hospitals. I watch as the nurse attaches sticky electrodes all over me because they want to make sure I'm not having a heart attack.

Trying to ignore the pain in my chest and left arm, my mind ran frantically, trying to rationalise what was happening. Surely this was just gas or something stupid. A heart attack? No. How could I be having a heart attack? I wasn't old enough.

I stared at the fluorescent ceiling light, mottled through my steamed glasses. The room was green and vinyl. It reminded me of Scotland, Ward 3B and everything that came with it. I just wanted to scream and run out of the building.

Instead, I sat silently, screaming internally as the nurse finished up ready to run the ECG. I closed my eyes, I felt something hot and angry running down my cheeks. Within that darkness, I tried to ignore my painful breathing and tried to accept the reality of why I was in this hospital, and this position.

It was my fault.

For the first time in my life, I had let someone get the better of me. *Look what I had let them do to me.* My mind went quiet, as I lay still and sniffled quietly feeling the shame overwhelm me.

I've spoken at length about some of the terrible managers I've had previously, but firmly thought that these belonged as cautionary tales in the past.

As my career progressed, and the IPCC became the IOPC, I worked hard and climbed the corporate ladder. When I got to a certain level, I really didn't expect that sort of nonsense again, naively perhaps. I'd got to a position where I thought *"finally"*, I'm safe here, enjoying the view from what I thought was the summit, unspoiled and beautiful.

I couldn't have been more wrong.

Marmite.

You either love it or you hate it. That was the phrase coined internally for my latest manager who joined a while after I had been placed in post as Director for London.

"They are very marmite Sal. It's just them, it's their style, their personality."

And that was some personality. After barely a couple of weeks into their role, the mask didn't just slip, it fell off and shattered into a million pieces.

In all of my years working in professional environments I had *never* been spoken to in the way that this individual spoke to me. It was awful, far worse than any other manager I'd had previously. It soon became clear to me that an entire career had been built on that personality. In the way they spoke to people, in the way they treated people, in the way they left people feeling. They trod on people, the broken souls of those underneath building a staircase all the way to the top.

They were clever and vindictive in equal measure.

I had regular monthly one-to-one meetings with them, and increasingly didn't look forward to these meetings because of the very fact I was alone in their company. It didn't feel safe.

On one occasion I was working in the bedroom where unknowingly, the door was slightly ajar. My wife was in the room next door and could hear the conversation playing out. Working from home, my wife was very used to me making calls, the sound of corporate chitter chatter was our background noise between the hours of 9 and 5. That day, the call ended, and I felt tired. As I left the room my wife caught me and asked who I was speaking to. I said it had been a meeting with my manager. She paused and said:

"*Your manager speaks to you like that*?"
I just nodded. She was furious and I was just embarrassed, and ashamed

Regardless, I still wanted to do my best. I'd worked hard to get to where I was, and I wanted to do a good job of it, so I put on my coat of armour and carried on. The harder I worked, and the more I brought to the table in the way I managed, the way I work and the way I operate outside the typical groupthink, the more they placed obstacles in front of me.

At the level I was working at, that is actually quite a difficult thing to do, so it was never in an obvious way, it was always underhand. It meant that rather than saying a straight *'no'* to something I might want to do or might be doing, they would ensure it was the actual corporate process that would be changed entirely to prevent me carrying on. That *'no'* was then a product of the corporate policy carefully machinated to stifle me. Very specifically me.

This was no more apparent than in events surrounding Reverend Mina Smallman, the mother of Bibaa Henry and Nicole Smallman.

287

The police handling of the case had already drawn wide criticism, and rightly so. On reporting their daughters missing, the treatment of the family had been absolutely appalling. As such, it was being investigated independently. A case which was absolutely horrendous in itself, was somehow made even worse by the uncovering of two selfies, taken at the murder scene by the two serving police officers who had been put in place to *protect* it. This became a criminal matter after the Crown Prosecution Service made the decision to charge.

It was building up to the court date, and I was preparing for the fact that I'd be making what is referred to as a *'steps of court statement'*. This is a statement given to the press normally by the legal team and family, as they leave court for the final time. These statements are made at the end of what can be a gruelling, painful legal process. A steps of court statement is one of the only opportunities for those involved in the case to speak their truth to the press, and the public. In this particular instance, I was working with a comms officer to draft a statement on behalf of the IOPC. In light of the horror that Mina Smallman and her family had already endured, I didn't want this just to be a 'statement on behalf of an IOPC spokesperson'. I wanted it to be human. Nothing that would prejudice our independence, but something that was appropriate given the circumstances. I wanted to acknowledge the depravity of the actions of these officers, the pain that Mina Smallman and her family had suffered, and the cultural change that was quite clearly needed within policing. I was in a position where I could help to influence that change, and given the disgraceful actions of these officers? I wasn't going to let that pass. I wanted to say what needed to be said, in the way it needed to be.

Guess who didn't like it?

Marmite, of course. They disliked it fiercely.

We met to discuss it; the press officer already upset at the treatment they themselves had suffered at the hands of marmite. I stood my ground on the fact that this was what needed to be said and, in this instance, it was my call to make. That went down even better than the statement, which was something I'd find out later had consequences for me.

The day arrived, and it was hard. Job aside, it was a *really* hard day. Watching in the dock as these two officers who had done a despicable thing were given a custodial sentence, and not an insignificant one either. I thought an element of me would be satisfied, but I wasn't. It was just sadness. The pain that this family had gone through, the waste of these two police officers' lives and careers, the pain for their families who were watching on, and for what?

I showed Reverend Smallman and her family what I planned to say, because I wanted to be respectful, and then I delivered those words to the best of my ability. Twenty odd cameras thrust in my face, frenzied lights flashing. None of that mattered. I just wanted to deliver words that did that horror, and family justice.

As I finished, Mina Smallman touched me on the shoulder and whispered, *"Thank you."*

That meant a lot, it still does.

Then, she herself took to the steps with a level of bravery I will never fully understand. A bereaved mother, with no notes, eviscerated the Met for everything that had happened and called out its leadership. No one else could have delivered it in the way that she did; with power, with poise and with grace.

I came back to work the next day and there was no uproar. No public outcry, no negative press coverage on what I'd said. But there were a couple of royally fucked off people who were not at all happy.

I couldn't understand why, I still don't actually. What followed was one of the only instances of, I would argue, of Government interference to our independence that I witnessed during my time at that organisation. A Minister at the Home Office had apparently expressed their displeasure regarding my statement, with a particular issue around the use of the word 'disgusting'. I don't consider that an unreasonable word when you look at what these officers did. In fact, I think it was quite mild.

Once it had been fed back that the Minister was unhappy with the statement, people all around me started flapping. There was a phrase circulating on behalf of that Minister which I can't recall, that talked to the issue my statement had apparently raised. So, guess what happened next? Yep, a policy change. Actually, two policy changes.

Firstly, the policy around the steps of court statements was changed entirely, banning these taking place, weeks after I had made mine. Secondly, there was the introduction of a new *'tone of voice'* policy for any communications with the media, which was all centred rather unbelievably around the particular phrase the Minister had used to express their earlier displeasure.

Let me be clear, I was the only person at that organisation regularly speaking to the media at the time, so that was basically a change of *my* tone of voice when speaking externally. Reflecting on that now, I still think it's deeply problematic for an independent body to take such a strong steer from a senior politician and to make that organisational policy change.

My manager helped put into motion these changes, along with another senior manager who was also a huge part of the problem at the IOPC. It was wildly counterproductive at the time, because in the job I was doing I was really starting to find my voice in talking to the issues that needed to be spoken about. Race discrimination, disproportionately within policing, issues that have plagued communities for decades. I was trying so hard to get those issues the airtime they needed and deserved.

Increasingly, I was being blocked. Everything I said was monitored and micro-managed to suffocating levels. Eventually, I think out of concern, a trusted colleague approached me and made it clear that actually, there was jealousy around the coverage I was getting.

Despite the fact that what I was doing the right thing, and what needed to be done, there was jealousy that it was me on the podium and not them.

The increasing pressure was being felt by me, in a way that I didn't appreciate at that time. Our one-to-one conversations continued in the same vein. Sessions that should be open conversations around workload, welfare and development opportunities were actually a good hour used to tear me to shreds and point out how shit I was at my job. As in any abusive relationship, I really began to doubt myself until eventually I found myself checking in with trusted colleagues to see if I really *was* shit at my job, but they all said otherwise, which to me was a revelation. Communities and stakeholders who had initially greeted me with extreme and justified caution were backing the work I was trying to do and me, personally.

So, I kept on my coat of armour, and I pushed
ahead.

The abuse continued, that circling sense of
suffocation that had me in its grasp day in, day
out. As I fought on, the attempts to block me
appeared to be getting more and more
desperate.

My diary was being monitored, closely. This
really senior person, spending significant time
checking my diary to see what I was doing, and
when. Meetings would be queried; timings would
be questioned. As an abusive relationship, it
really was textbook. On one occasion, there was
an attempt to stop me from going to a
conference because we 'already had
representation'. I had to point out that I was a
keynote speaker at that conference, so I kinda'
needed to be there.

After that, things were cranked things up a notch
to make my life a misery. It worked.
Out of straws to clutch *inside* of work, my
movements were controlled in a way that would
impact my life *outside* of work. Suddenly, I found
myself being told that I couldn't be involved in
certain things because of my 'childcare
requirements'. Annual leave was being blocked

for 'business reasons'. I was being penalised quite openly for having a family and parental responsibilities.
That was the straw that broke the camel's back. I wasn't having it.

I made it very clear that if that was the rule *I* needed to follow, that was the role *everyone* needed to follow. I absolutely refused to accept it, any of it. The more I pushed back, the more resistance I got. But, thanks to HR policy, it couldn't be argued either.

Until my next one to one.

It was October 2021, the morning of my one to one, and as had become the pattern, I was absolutely dreading it. I'd been putting it off for a while. I knew I would be walking into an absolute barrage of spewed, pent up frustration and bile, despite the fact that I was working really hard and doing the best job that I could in what was a historically difficult time for policing and the Met in particular.
The dread I felt that day was different, I actually didn't feel well.

I loosened my collar and took a seat; my legs and hands were shaking. My chest was getting tighter and, as breathing became more difficult, shooting pains started to go down my left arm. I did the usual man thing, I ignored it, because that tactic works well. But it didn't go away. I felt my face flush with panic as my heart rate quickened and the reality of the situation hit me.

Somehow, I still felt the need to email my boss to explain that I was having chest pains and wouldn't make our call. I know how crazy that sounds looking at the situation now, but that was how I was working at the time. That was how indoctrinated I had become.

I told my wife I didn't feel well and was going to the hospital, I didn't want anyone to worry so I didn't make a fuss and, although she wanted to come, I insisted it was fine and that I was just going as a precaution.
I then called an Uber and headed to the hospital in a state of confusion, and unusually, I was afraid.

I'd been waiting in the hospital for five hours.

This was right in the midst of Covid, and that additional factor just made the whole experience horrible. Although the waiting time was lengthy, the nurses were keeping an eye on me because of the symptoms I'd described. I can't remember much about that period, except for keeping my wife updated via WhatsApp.

I do remember one thing I did at the time. I took a selfie.

I took it as a reminder of that moment in time, the moment when I was sat in that grey hospital waiting room, struggling to breathe properly. This was my lowest moment at work, almost ever, actually. I had to be able to remember this so that I could make sure this never happened again. I still don't quite understand the fact that I did this. It wasn't until two years later in writing this book that I looked at this photo again and remembered.

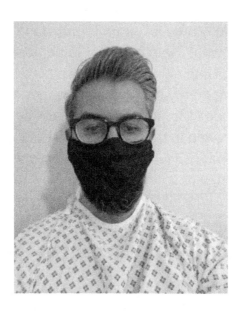

I look awful, I felt awful, and I share this photo not to evoke any sympathy from anyone, but simply to show you the face of what can happen when a toxic manager reigns inside a toxic culture, unchallenged.

It's people that suffer, and I don't want anyone else to suffer.
The nurses did their tests and given my symptoms, took a long while to rule out a heart attack, even taking bloods. Eventually they concluded that it was a really bad panic attack, grilling me about how much stress I was under at work. I ended up being really honest.

They had finally got me.

Heading home, I was on autopilot and my mind was blank. I was still in pain, I felt awful but couldn't fully process or understand the true extent of what I was feeling. I remember sinking into what I can only describe as a black hole. I'd been wearing my coat of inner armour for too long. I hadn't listened to my own advice of knowing when to take it off and get out of the fight for fear of injury, which is exactly what had happened. It had affected me deeply.

There was no way I was in any fit state to go back to work. The thought of that alone made me feel unwell. I ended up being off work for the next two months. The first time in my life I had been off sick with stress. I went from a person who doesn't take sick days to someone who fell into that managerial terminology of *'long-term sick'*.

I resented that. I *really* resented that someone had gone to such vindictive lengths to make my life unbearable, and for what? Because I was good at my job?

As I spent time at home, reflecting on what had happened to me, thoughts filled my mind as to why they had felt such a need to destroy me. It was a horrible time because I was fighting against myself and admitting my own need to recover. They had managed to break me, and I was struggling to accept what my body was telling me. I couldn't fathom what I had done to deserve this which had been *that* bad.

I'll be honest, it did cross my mind. Is it a race thing? Is that what it is? Is that what it's always been? Still to this day, I don't know. But do I think I was treated differently?

Absolutely.

But *why* did they treat me in the way they did? I'll never be able to square that circle. And actually, I don't care to. Here, yes, I had anger, but that anger was actually directed toward myself. I had let someone get the better of me and I was so angry that was the case because it had never happened before. This was on me, that was what I thought.
And rightly or wrongly, that's still my view today.

Eventually, I did go back. I didn't know if it was the right thing to do, but I did know that under no circumstances would I work under that individual again, and I didn't.

Like a bone that had been broken when I came back, I was stronger, it took me a few weeks to find my rhythm again but then I had Operation Hotton. I approached that with a real fire inside me. I was determined to do what needed to be done to put that out into the public glare, and under the spotlight that it needed. No one was going to stop me.

I look back now and wonder, if I *hadn't* fallen when I did, and had the time to recharge and reflect, would I have had it in me to do that?

Would I have stood my ground in publishing the text messages that laid the Met bare for all to see?
Would I have opened a can that effectively led to the resignation of the then Met Commissioner?

Would I have put onto paper, on the world stage, just why change is so badly needed within the culture of British policing?

I don't know, but I'd like to think yes, I would have.

That experience, and the ones that preceded it, were meant for me. I truly believe that, and as always, I thank God for the good and the bad. Perhaps at that time, I needed that grounding, a reminder of what other people have to face and who, seniority aside, the person I am. It was a humbling reminder that no matter how senior you get, no matter how hard you work, how much you are paid, you can still fall foul to people who are that entrenched in power that they seek to destroy others for their own perverse reasons. It was a valuable lesson. Never again would I take on a role and assume any level of safety by virtue of my title and position alone.

Bullying and some of the workplace toxicity that people talk of as the exception? For me, more often than not has been my norm. In writing this book and revisiting some of those experiences, I've been keen to look into that further, to try and understand why.

Recently, I came across an article which helps sheds some light here. The article focuses on people who are self-directed, something I would consider myself to be because of the values-led way I operate. I've always supported my managers and tried to have their back when needed, but not if it clashes with my own core values, my own true north. I've always been sure of myself in that sense. The article spoke to the fact that insecure managers feel threatened by that way of working, which really struck a chord. It started to make sense to me, and this passage was the killer:

"The most likely target of workplace bullying is the kind of worker many employers dream of: workers who are highly self-sufficient, judicious, and creative, and who demonstrate internal motivation, possess a benevolent worldview, and refrain from office politics and one-upmanship. In a word, the self-directed."

I look back now and wonder, how did I get through some of that stuff? Because even writing and remembering it has been quite difficult. Equipping myself with the necessary knowledge was key, which meant having an intimate working knowledge of all of the relevant HR policies. This enabled a level of empowerment and confidence in navigating the internal decision tree, and which route to follow and with whom to speak.

I remember speaking at great length in the aftermath of Op Hotton about culture, and how it has the power to make or break an organisation, and the people within it. People didn't know it at the time, but I was speaking from my very recent, very personal experience here.

I was a victim as well, but until I put pen to paper, I had never realised that before. Exceptional leadership actually requires the very simplest of things. The best leaders I've met are kind. Kindness is something that is really underrated and something that I really try to embody. They lead with courage, doing the right thing *because it's the right thing.*

They are fair. They are values-led and understand intimately their true north.

Real leaders have no ego; they don't need to. Some of the best leaders I've met have no fancy title, they earn respect in the way they act, the way they treat people, and the way they make people feel.

Some of these exceptional leaders are quoted on the covers of this book, because their leadership and character was something I admired hugely when I encountered it in my work in professional life.

An organisation who totally gets that, is Timpsons. You know the store on the High St that cuts keys for homes around the country and dry-cleans coats for the masses? They operate with kindness. Not just in some wishy-washy mission statement that sits on their website, they operate with kindness - in action. If you're homeless and have a job interview? Don't mention it, they'll dry clean your clothes for free and wish you luck on your next chapter. They hire large numbers of rehabilitated offenders who want and deserve a second chance at life, without prejudice.

Every year, like many other organisations, they send out a staff survey. Unlike any staff survey I've ever seen; it contains only one question:

How do you rate your leader?

They totally get it, understanding the leadership quotient in your organisation is the key to everything.

Until more organisations grasp this essential point, good leadership will occur in your career more randomly than by design. The type of terrible leadership I've described has consequences but also is more common than we as individuals might appreciate.

According to a groundbreaking study[41] by the Chartered Management Institute (CMI) in partnership with YouGov, one in three people, both managers and workers, have left their jobs due to a negative work culture. The impact of bad management extends beyond job satisfaction, it affects motivation and the likelihood of people leaving. Shockingly, 82% of workers entering management positions have not received any formal management and leadership training, contributing to the UK's stock of 'accidental managers'.

---

[41] New study: Bad managers and toxic work culture causing one in three staff to walk - CMI

This is the scale of this hidden problem. Until organisations wake up to this there will continue to be this churn, and in cases like mine, human collateral as a consequence. People deserve good leadership; it shouldn't be the exception. Workplace cultures need to stop acting as apologists for despot managers, excusing terrible behaviour as it being a question of an acquired taste. An acquired taste like, umm, Marmite? That's doing a massive disservice to Marmite.

Having said that…fucking awful stuff isn't it?

Chapter 10
Poking the bear

*"You shall judge a man by his foes as well
as by his friends."*

Joseph Conrad

"You need to be careful Sal."

Toward the end of my time at the IOPC, I heard
this several times from serving officers in the
Met.

These weren't officers based in New Scotland
Yard, they were more junior but arguably more
important grades performing that impossible job
on the frontline. I used to meet these officers
when I spoke at events in my role as the
National Discrimination Lead for my
organisation. I used these inputs to speak to the
difficult issues and call out the elephants in the
room:

- The lack of racial diversity at the most
  senior ranks of policing, there has only

307

been one Chief Constable of colour in the history of UK policing.

- The lack of attention the issue of racism received in policing whether that was internally in its own culture or baked into certain policing tactics such as stop and search

- The lack of acknowledgment of the scale of misogyny faced by female police officers within their own forces.

All my inputs were carefully crafted and rooted in evidence to navigate my way through the internal machinery of resistance of my own organisation, to then poke the internal machinery of resistance in policing. Poking the bear essentially. It wasn't easy speaking on these topics when some in the audience were very clear that they didn't want you there. But easy was irrelevant. It was always about trying to make the most of the opportunity I had at the time.

There was always a strange thing that happened when I spoke, every time I would come off stage the female officers and the officers of colour would approach me afterwards. We would walk off into some quiet corner and they would then go on to recount their own horrible experiences. They were victims. It was always hard to hear these stories, and they would be on their own sliding scale of gristle. In most cases, they just wanted to tell me, to share with someone who they thought might *'get it'*. In one or two other cases I tried my best to help.

I always noticed that the White male officers never approached me afterwards.

I wished they had, but perhaps it's a hard thing to do when implicit in everything I was saying on those stages was criticism of White men. Or perhaps some were conscious of the optics of engaging with the "enemy" and felt the peer pressure of not going there? With hindsight, it's something I should have examined more closely at the time and thought about. "How do I better get them engaged on these issues?"

As I've mentioned, my routine was to engage with those senior officers based at New Scotland Yard, however on several occasions I met with officers from the Met, who were outside of this senior rank structure and this very weird thing happened - they thanked me. I'm the IOPC, in theory, for police officer`s, I'm the *bogeyman*, this shouldn't really happen. I want to protect their confidence so what I will say in general terms is that they used to tell me that I had the senior leadership team worried, and that they were supporting me all the way.

Supporting *me.*

That was quite the thing to process.

That these officers, who were the victims of this toxic culture in parts of the Met were actually supporting me. I had gotten so used to having my head down, and fighting my own lonely battle inside the IOPC that never did I think at any point I might I have some support, or anyone had noticed what I was trying to do.

And yes, I did.

But some had.

So yes, they also warned me to be careful. I remember after a couple of separate times hearing the warnings from these officers about watching my back feeling like someone had given me an unwanted gift and I had no idea what to do with it. One evening I told my wife; I think almost to say out loud what had been said to me but that was it. I then remembered what happened to Jennifer Izekor.

Jennifer Izekor was a former commissioner of the Independent Police Complaints Commission (IPCC). She was exonerated of allegations related to evidence suppression in the case of a Black firefighter Tasered by Met officers after the 2011 riots. The investigation, known as Operation Amherst, was conducted by Police Scotland, took over four years and cost taxpayers more than £1.5 million. After four long years she was cleared. The evidence revealed that the Met had possession of crucial disclosures all along.

In a later interview with the Guardian Jennifer said[42] :

"I remember one of the officers I was working with was bringing a case against [the Met], and his career had been destroyed in the way that the Baroness Casey Review sets out," she said. "And he said to me, very distinctly:" Jennifer, you keep going like this and they will clear your legs." It was the first time I heard the phrase.

---

[42] Watchdog commissioner says Met sabotaged her career over investigations of racism | Metropolitan police | The Guardian

And I said:" What does that mean?" And he said," That's what happens if you go up against the Met, they'll take you out." I said," No, I'm a public servant, They wouldn't do that to me. That came back to haunt me."

Jennifer Izekor is a Black woman. A fact that just cannot be lost here.

So, in what was being said to me by these officers, the Met had form here. But I basically ignored this.

Not to dismiss it, but really because *what could I do about it*? My conscience was clean. and I was always following the evidence through my role, which led to the public positions that I articulated. There was also zero point in me sharing this internally within the IOPC, I just didn't have the trust or confidence to have that sort of conversation internally with the senior leadership team. So, I just carried on in the way that I always had and accepted that this was a consequence of what happens when you poke the bear. I carried on with those words *without fear or favour* ringing loudly in my ears.

Later on, I had it on good authority that two very senior officers in the Met didn't like me, I mean really disliked me. I then smiled as I remembered what all of those officers had told me.

Is it wrong that I took that as a type of compliment?

Maybe.

But that's exactly what I did, because as far as I was concerned these two particular individuals were part of the problem. They were part of the moral decay in leadership standards I witnessed in my tenure in Scotland Yard, where too many of these *leaders'* moral alignment was never right in my eyes, about the issues at stake. It was always about protecting the brand that is the Met and living in this *Narnia-esque* bubble of denial about what was actually going on.

If this was the barometer, of those not liking me inside the Met, arguably I was performing my job in the right way.

In New Scotland Yard I found the lack of moral courage to address the elephants in the room and call things out in the way that they needed to be called out, astonishing. Police officers perform such difficult roles, and so many display values-led leadership pretty much every day on the frontline, so it was curious to me that when I faced and interacted with the senior echelons of the Met I was always left wondering when in their career they had made those compromises in their values, to end up in the position that I found them in. Was it a process of erosion? Or was it just a conscious choice they'd made along the way?

No idea, but this was what I was left dealing with. Yes, it wasn't everybody, but it was too many. Too many morally hollowed-out, alleged senior leaders of policing.

I remember asking in one meeting when there were three senior officers present, and I had a long list of horrific cases which we were independently investigating, out of sheer frustration at the tenor of the meeting:

"Aren't you all worried about what you`re seeing?"

I looked at them on my screen naively waiting for an answer.

They looked at me.

There was silence.

They weren't going to answer. That day my face couldn't hide my disgust. Why did I feel so strongly? It's probably worth highlighting some of the cases I was dealing with at the time:

- Child Q: the strip search of a child on her period for drugs by officers who had been called to her school
- Jordan Walker Brown: The tasering of a young Black man fleeing from the police which left with him paralysed
- Nicole Smallman & Bibba Henry- Two officers who has taken selfies at the murder scene of these two young Black women
- Stephen Port: The failings in the investigation of the murders of several young gay men which allowed a serial killer to evade justice.
- Sarah Everhard: The murder of this young woman by Wayne Couzens a serving officer in the Met at the time.
- Bianca Williams & Ricard Dos Santos- The high profile stop and search of two young Black athletes.

- David Carrick: A serving officer of the Met who would be later found to guilty of 24 counts of rape.
- Operation Hotton

These were just some of the cases, there were many more. Which is why I wore the look of disgust that I did on that day.

And as I moved the conversation on, I let that look speak for itself.

A telling fact from my time at the IOPC as Director for London was, that I only ever had one face to face meeting with the Commissioner, at the time this was Dame Cressida Dick. I say telling, because the hierarchy the organisation permitted inside the IOPC meant I was essentially never deemed senior enough to have these meetings - it would fall to the then Director General. It is also my strong view this was something the Met managed very effectively in my organisation by creating this hierarchy where essentially my senior contact with them was *managed*. However, one time I did meet the Commissioner - then Dame Cressida Dick, albeit it was to accompany my Director General, while she had her Deputy Assistant Commissioner present.

We were meeting the Commissioner after Op Hotton, and she was in the process of leaving the Met after resigning. I honestly can't remember the purpose of the meeting, but I was to find out later why I was there. In all my time at the IPCC/IOPC I never met anyone that worked for, or with, the Commissioner that had a bad word to say about her. Not one. That always stuck with me, because that did mean something and also revealed an awful lot about her leadership style. But this juxtaposition of her inter-personal leadership style with that of the Metropolitan Police jarred.

To me it was evident that she wasn't willing to readily hear criticism of her officers. Now that quality of loyalty is to be absolutely admired, but not when it's *blind* loyalty and from my vantage point I saw that was the case far too often. The latter actually proved harmful to her own organisation.

When I met the Commissioner, I couldn't help but like her. She came across really well, much more human than most of her senior leadership team. There was a genuine warmth to her. I also watched how she interacted with her people, and how they reacted to her. You could see the relationship was there.

Having said that, it wasn't a particularly easy meeting for me. It turned out that I had been brought to that meeting by the Director General to talk about our decision on the independent investigation featuring Bianca Willams and her partner, Ricardo Dos Santos. The conversation had been convivial up until then, and nothing really I think which would be fair to share, but this part I do think is worth including because it was so revealing of the attitude within the highest level of seniority in the Met regarding the issues of racism and stop and search.

When we came on to talk about this investigation it was evident the Commissioner wanted to air her grievances on my position as the decision maker, remembering at the start of this she had said the officers had done nothing wrong here. Her concern was that our position was that all officers conducting stop and search were at a starting point of racial bias.

The Director General looked at me to respond, evidently wanting to avoid having the difficult conversation, and so I did.

I stated pretty curtly this wasn't the case at all, we had *never* said this anywhere, and this thinking wasn't contained in any of my decision making. Essentially, I called bullshit. I went on to explain how I had found evidence of racial bias detected in the behaviours of some of those officers, detailing some of this. Not overt racist remarks, but racism that I believed could be evidenced in how this young Black man and woman had been treated differently during the stop and search. A starting position that all officers conducting stop and search were racially biased was stuff of fantasy from the Commissioner and the Met. Frankly her even saying this to me was as alarming as it was insightful to their stance on these issues. *This* is what they had taken from this incredibly high-profile stop and search and our investigation. Zero desire to actually learn and improve on what had become such a contentious matter, and a totem on the issues around stop and search faced by Black communities across London. Only a desire to push back and tell me why I was wrong.

When I pointed out to the Commissioner that after two years her team had at the very end altered their position and agreed with me that two of the officers involved did have a case to answer for gross misconduct, her face turned. She looked at her Deputy Assistant Commissioner sat across from her, who shifted uncomfortably in her seat. The Commissioner clearly didn't know.

I didn't say anything, and just soaked up the awkwardness of that moment. Our meeting ended shortly after that.

It was my only meeting with Commissioner Dick, and initially I resisted the temptation to draw anything out of it because of that very fact, it was just one meeting, but in retrospect there was something there. That something being, it was a tiny microcosm of the issues at play in the Met at the time, the tension between her personal and organisational leadership, the lack of understanding about racial bias, the unwavering support for stop and search and that instinct to deny the reality of the problem needed to be faced and to instead push back.

As I walked out of New Scotland Yard that day, I was thinking about how important it was that I continued to keep to my values when performing my role, whether that bear reared up or not, intimidation wasn't an option. I was also wondering if the new Commissioner, who had yet to be appointed, would fall into these same traps.

I hoped not.

For the sake of all those officers inside the Met whose horrific stories I had heard, for the sake of those members of the public who had suffered the consequences of the toxic culture inside parts of the Met, and for the sake of those Londoners who just didn't have any trust left in this police service and deserved so much better.

Chapter 11

The park bench

"The wonder is not that so many are ruined but that so many survive."

James Baldwin

I was hearing the words come out of my mouth, but not quite believing what I was saying.

It was February 2023, it was sunny, and the cold was cutting through me.

I was speaking to the occupational health adviser that had been assigned to me, who I could hear speak more and more haltingly as I gave my answers to her scripted questions. The phone pressed hard to my ear, I sat myself on a park bench in Victoria Embankment Gardens, overlooking an austere Whitehall building and fixing my gaze on one of the many bronzed memorial statutes which circled the park.

It wasn't the first time I'd been there. I used to go and sit there sometimes if I was early for a visit to New Scotland Yard, as the park was right beside it. It was always a welcome breather ahead of whatever gristly conversation I needed to have with whichever senior officer I was meeting at the time. It was a chance to see a bit of greenery during my urban sprint, and to take in a bit of the history.

On this day in particular, I was waiting to go into New Scotland Yard, for a meeting with Baroness Louise Casey and her team.

She was conducting her independent review into the Met and wanted to speak to me as part of that. Much to my amusement, her team had made clear it was only me Baroness Casey wanted to speak to. I say amusement as I knew several senior egos were pricked by this not-so-subtle rebuttal.

Ahead of what was going to be a significant meeting, why was I speaking to the occupational health adviser just before going in? Because it was the only time I could fit that conversation into my diary and because after what I had told my organisation, they had insisted I speak to someone, quickly.

They were worried.

Something wasn't right.

It had been an intense time at the IOPC, which is probably understating things. Latterly, I was the decision-maker in the independent investigation into the fatal shooting of Chris Kaba on 5 September 2022. A case that made my heart sink when I heard all of the circumstances. It's a case I'll refrain from sharing my full thoughts right now, because at the time of writing this there is a pending murder trial concerning the Met firearm's officer, following my team's independent investigation.

But there are two moments from this investigation which I want to mention at this time:

The two scenarios which stuck with me were firstly the family's reaction and between them and their solicitor, the compelling need they felt to keep the pressure on us because painfully they had so little faith in us. The IOPC was in place for this very scenario. In theory to provide confidence to bereaved families where there had been a death following the use of lethal force by the police that a robust independent investigation would be completed. And yet, because of past failures in the timeliness of investigations which had taken years, they felt the need to do this. They had no confidence in us. I found that quite a difficult thing to accept because all I and my team wanted to do was to get to the truth of what happened here, and I wanted to tell the family this, but I knew that my words would just sound hollow against their sadly justified cynicism. This just added another question I had on this whole system I was operating in.

The second moment which I wanted to mention was again during the difficult first week of that investigation. During my time at the IOPC I had developed good working relationships with many people, because I think people got that I was genuinely trying to make a difference. One of those people was Abimbola Johnson. Abi is an award-winning human rights barrister and commentator, but I knew her from her work as the Chair of the Independent Scrutiny and Oversight Board for the Police Race Action Plan. During this week Abi was interviewed by BBC Radio 4 for her thoughts on the investigation and in this interview she did something which I'll never forget, naming me and saying she had faith in me and therefore the investigation that would be conducted by the IOPC. It was fed back to me later, and it was quite the thing to process because the IOPC wasn't held in high regard amongst the communities of London and here was someone who had effectively risked her own reputation to state their confidence in me. It was a gesture that cut through at that time and has stayed with me long afterwards.

And for many other reasons, it's an investigation I'll never forget.

I had always loved the work and believed in my purpose within it. That had been at my core and enabled me to pursue with whatever capacity I had for change within the Kafkaesque bureaucracy that was the police complaints system. It was something that had always been solid and unshakeable, or so I thought.

How we conducted ourselves at the IOPC had to be of a higher standard, just by virtue of what we were in place to do, in looking at how the police service held themselves to their professional standards.

But that wasn't always reflected internally in the behaviour of many of the people I worked with.

There was a culture where once a particular grade was passed, it came with an increased internal tolerance to toxicity, many looking the other way to poor behaviour. Unfortunately, I had to work alongside a few of these clowns, but never mind, I could see the joke.

However, when I became aware that one of these clowns had gone beyond the usual toxic circus act, it was no longer funny.

Allegations of misogyny came to my door; allegations that left me shocked and concerned enough to do something about it. I went down the whistleblowing route to raise my concerns, as I was worried for the welfare of more junior members of staff and knew this route would force the correct response. Or so I thought. The organisation's tepid response showed me ultimately a lack of moral courage. This surprised me, disappointed me, and enraged me in equal measure. I knew what needed to happen, and it didn't. Who were we if we couldn't deal with this properly? Did we just reserve our ire for policing and not ourselves? Shouldn't we be treating this with the same severity as we did with policing? I was left with these questions but no answers, and I couldn't do a thing about it.

So that was one thing that had taken a sizeable chunk out of me, and my core. I also remember a remark taking an equally large chunk, winding me in the process.

It was during a meeting with Bianca Williams and Ricardo Dos Santos, their lawyer, and my team. We were coming to the end of our investigation into their complaint about the stop and search. I was explaining the position I had reached, and we were speaking about what would happen next. At this stage I had made my decision that five of the officers had a case to answer for Gross Misconduct. The conversation went on to timescales and the separate, independent misconduct panel that would take place. Once I had gone through that Ricardo turned to me and said:

"So, what you`re saying is that my son, who was just a baby at the time this happened will probably be starting school by the time these officers face their hearing?"

All I could do was nod apologetically, and quietly say yes.

In one simple question, he encapsulated the entire problem with the system. The system that

I was working in. The system that I was part of. This was despite me doing everything possible in this investigation to try and do the right thing, and the personal cost, this was what the system led to. Both of these complainants had to await that outcome, had to have that level of endurance of stamina in their legitimate pursuit of accountability. They had done nothing wrong here, and yet the system demanded this emotional tax from them as the price to see this through to the end.

How could that be right?

It was something that really troubled me. I had always known it of course, but it's the human condition isn't it, that until you can get up close and see something for yourself your capacity for true understanding tends to be more limited? It was the way Ricardo had framed it, and just left it as an open hanging question. It wasn't right, we both knew that, and I couldn't do anything about it.

The meeting ended, but the impact of what he'd said didn't.

It followed me.

As did the reaction of Chris Kaba's family.

Then we had the sudden resignation of the Director General of the IOPC at the beginning of December 2022. I remember seeing an email being circulated internally that he had resigned, it was out of the blue on a Friday afternoon. Then in the weekend press I read a statement by the Home Secretary and found out just like everyone else that he was subject to a police investigation for *historical allegations*.[43]

I went numb. I struggled to process it.
Here was someone who I had worked with really well, who I had respected for their previous work with the families in Grenfell and who I considered to be an ally in the workplace. And yet, here they were now under investigation on what I was speculating, spoke to the very work the IOPC was intent on outing around male violence against women and girls in policing. Again, that issue had found its way not just to the door of the IOPC, but inside, to the very heart of the organisation,

I didn't want this to be true, because it would mean everything that I knew about this man and

---

[43] Police watchdog head Michael Lockwood resigns amid investigation - BBC News

his work would be tarnished. At that time there was no more information to make any more sense of it.

I remember going into work on that Monday; everyone was feeling it and processing it in their own way. Disbelief, anger, upset, denial, you could take your pick. I remember I was one of the few senior people who had to front up that day and still carry on with their public engagement. I was in City Hall that evening at an event hosted by the London Mayor's office. The easy thing to have done would have been to make my excuses and not attend, but that didn't feel right, and why should I? I had to front up and do what I always did, even though everything had changed.

And this was my point, everything had changed. We no longer had any credibility, we just didn't, and it didn't matter how anyone dressed it up. The IOPC was charged with the statutory purpose of independently investigating police misconduct without fear or favour, and to help improve public confidence in policing. How could we sincerely speak to this agenda now?

Whatever legitimacy we were trying to build crumbled.

And yet we had to carry on, and I did by attending that function at City Hall that Monday evening. I was dreading it. All I was going to do was be honest and focus on the work, what else could I do in that position? I remember walking into the foyer, not nervous but just bracing myself for the inevitable, and truthfully, justifiable reaction from people.

Then something unexpected happened.

People were asking if I was ok. One after the other. They were all being kind. It took my breath away, just that essential reminder of the capacity of kindness which exists in everyone, and what that feels like when you need it. It felt like an electric shock because I generally didn't feel it inside my own organisation. So, where I had braced myself in the anticipation of having a difficult evening, instead I was reminded that because people knew me for the work I did, and the change I tried to lead in London, that resonance mattered.

In a weird way, and at a really difficult moment, it was a touching affirmation.

Although I carried on, and the organisation rallied and moved through this crisis, I was struggling. Not in some affected sense of trying to locate my purpose, but I was getting increasingly unhappy. There was a disconnection happening inside me between my values and those of the organisation. That dislocation was having a cancerous effect on me. It felt like I was slowly drowning. I was sinking into the water and all of my loved ones were oblivious, enjoying themselves as I could see them through the refracting light of the water. They didn't have a clue, but I was going down.

I couldn't shake it off or talk myself out of it. I was miserable because of a culmination of the above and an essential truth captured in three words.

I was exhausted.

I was.

I don't how, or when exactly it had happened, but it had. It was the net effect and consequence of everything I had been through in the past few years in my role. As durable as I thought I was, I wasn't. Being the tip of the spear and constantly fighting for everything, along with the disconnection between what I believed and the reality of the organisation and system I was working in had left my reserves depleted. I had nothing left in the tank.

Nothing.

That was a shit thing to admit to myself and it took some time, but I did reluctantly. Eventually, overcoming my own ego and pride to do that.

I was done.

That Christmas I spoke to my wife and talked through what I was feeling and what I wanted to do. I was going to resign and walk away. I didn't have a job, or anything lined up, which was hard. But I knew I couldn't be there anymore. This was what I wanted to do, but I have a family, and my actions have consequences for them so it's not a decision that I could, or would, make alone. My wonderful wife backed me the whole way, even though we were stepping into certain uncertainty.

When I went back, I spoke to a few people to let them know my intentions, and it was all sorted amicably. However, one of the things asked of me by HR was to take part in an Occupational

Health Assessment, organisational due diligence to conclude things.

Fair enough, if that's what it took to get things wrapped up.

I could hear my responses to the adviser but was struggling to comprehend what I was saying.

So was she, I think.
The cold was biting me now and the bench was becoming more uncomfortable. It had been 15 minutes into a 30-minute call, and I just wanted it to end.

If anyone has ever had to do one of these assessments at work, you'll know the drill. They are essentially going through the motions, testing your fitness for work. You go through a series of structured questions and rate yourself. In these ratings, in my responses and in my discussion with the adviser, it became clear to me how bad I was, and the toll the job had taken on my mental health. Responses, which I struggle to play back in my own mind, even now and with the distance and benefit of time.

That call didn't need to go on for the full 30 minutes, the adviser had heard enough. I took a moment, caught my breath, and stared at the bronze monument in front of me. I needed to get that quiet back in my head. Ten minutes before I needed to meet Baroness Casey.

I got up from the bench, my bag feeling heavier, and walked over to New Scotland Yard.

What had been scheduled to be a 30-minute meeting went on for nearly two hours. It's always strange when I meet people that know who I am, but for Baroness Casey and her team to know not only who I was, but know about the work I'd done and to be so complimentary toward me? On that particular day, it was a bit of balm for my wounded soul. I won't go into the detail of that discussion as tempting as it might be, except to say I shared honestly and openly all of my insight into the Met and the system.

There was a lot to say.

The Casey Review[44] was published in early March 2023, and it was seismic. Its findings

---

[44] The Baroness Casey Review | Metropolitan Police

showed that the Met had actually regressed since the failings identified in the Stephen Lawerence Inquiry. It concluded that not only was it still institutionally racist, but also now the review found it to be also institutionally misogynistic and homophobic. It was another historic moment, and the report was a validation of many of the issues I (and many others) had been speaking about for many years within the Met. To have played a tiny part in something that was so significant was a moment for pause and reflection, particularly as that was my last substantive act in my role as Director for London at the IOPC.

During my resignation the fact I wasn't in a normal job became very clear.
In one breath, some were patronising me saying it was to be treated the same as any other resignation of a staff member would be. On the other hand, a detailed stakeholder engagement plan was being developed to communicate the fact I was leaving the IOPC. Although I have to be grateful for the kindness of a few individuals, there were others who made that process a confirmation of why I needed to leave, as soon as possible. My patience was being tested as usual, but at a point where I had none.

My main concern was to tell my team, and the people I had worked closely with inside the organisation, and outside of the organisation, personally. That was what was important to me. I let the rest be.

When I was telling people, it was difficult because these were all people I respected and trusted, and some of them were upset. During this time, I spent a weekend penning my last email. I wanted it to be an honest representation of my own voice, and despite an attempt, no-one would be changing a single word in my email. An odd thought occurred to me as I was writing it, *what if this email gets leaked? Am I happy with everything I've written in here?* I have no idea why I thought that, probably because of some latent test I was applying to myself to make sure my message was cogent, because I knew the state I was in.

Turns out, that thought was pretty prescient.

On 16th Match 2023 I officially resigned and walked away from the IOPC.

What was always going to be an emotional day turned out to be even harder because of someone/some people inside my own organisation. My email was leaked to BBC Newsnight who then tried to infer the reason I was resigning was because of the story they had run. The absolute unbridled arrogance of it. It was then splashed on Twitter with people piling on. The journalist who had colluded with the LI then joined in the pile-on by publishing my full email on Twitter.

To save you searching here it is below:

Dear Team

I thought about many ways I could start this message, and never really nailed it because it's probably one of the most difficult emails I've had to write over the past few years.

I've made the decision to resign from my position as Regional Director for London and Strategic Lead on Discrimination.

I'm making this decision because sometimes life is about choices, no matter how difficult they are, and I've made the choice to prioritise my family, and myself, over my role.

I have no idea what the future holds, because when you`ve performed a role like the one I have, it's difficult to know what else can have the same potential for impact and difference. So, I`ll be taking a bit of time out and thinking about what I do next.

I'll always be proud to say I worked at the IOPC. I have tried my best to represent what in my mind a RD should be about over these past 4 years and had an unashamedly strong external focus, as I believed being independent didn't mean being invisible. So, I've always done my best to represent us in an authentic way publicly in the most difficult conversations, on the most difficult issues, in the most difficult spaces. There are many many pieces of work I am proud to have worked on, led, and represented. I feel proud to see the relevance we and our work have had over these past few years at such a critical time for police accountability and public confidence.

Performing my role has attracted its critics, because when you are prepared to bring your difference to the table, stick your head above the parapet, and you look like me, sadly there is always someone waiting there trying to take your head off…

…but I accepted that a long time ago as the price of staying true to my values.

My most precious memories are however of working with so many amazing colleagues. Because, when you drill down into it, and look beyond the strategies, the corporate plans, and the programmes of work - it is all about the people.

I can only play tribute to the incredible work done by everyone I have had the privilege to say has been on my team. I`ve seen this up close in the most incredibly difficult situations which often play out in the media and national stage. Everyone plays their part, ESO, ESM, ISU, Trainee Investigators, Investigators, Leads, OTLs, OMs….but, as I realised in my role that list doesn't stop there.

Over these past few years, I am also proud of all the work we have achieved in our thematic work on racial discrimination. For many reasons the work hasn't been easy, and yet my colleagues on the

Discrimination SMN have been absolutely immense.

To do our work means working hand in glove with different parts of the IOPC like, legal, comms, policy, stakeholder engagement, DMI, casework, assessment unit. But then there is also all the essential infrastructure which we all need to do our jobs like FM, IT, Finance, L&D, Performance, HR- and all the people that make that possible.

I'm sorry I haven't namechecked everyone or every team, but hopefully my sentiment comes across clearly, that each and every one of us plays our part.

This role has been the highlight of my professional working life, but I am and always was, just a custodian. I wish the next person who takes custodianship of this position every possible success and to realise how lucky they will be. Lucky, to occupy such an important position where every day should be filled with the possibility of what change they can make by working with such committed, passionate, brilliant people.

Special mention to; Rezwana, Scarlett, Uzma, Paulette, Colin, Neil, and Adam who have had to put up with me disproportionately and been there through thick and thin.

I'll be back in the office in a few weeks and hopefully then get a chance to say goodbye properly, but for today I'd like to say thank you.

You all make the incredibly important work of the IOPC possible.

You are its most precious asset.

And I was blessed to have worked with you.

Best wishes

Sal

I wasn't even allowed the dignity of resigning without one last attempt from those determined to break me. And that's my reading of this last act at its kindest, because another equally legitimate way of reading this was my own organisation was doing its best to finish me off.

At my lowest, this was my treatment from that system I had given everything to. Which I had in truth, given too much to.

I got some lovely emails and messages from some colleagues but truthfully, the reaction from those outside of the organisation is what I hold onto most from that day and that week. To feel that love from those that understood the work, in such respected positions, was feedback that I've now learned to accept in how I conducted my role.

One thing which bothers me about my leaving the IOPC, and that I didn't address at the time, was that at no point did anyone ask *why* I felt the way I did. *Why* did I feel exhausted? *Why* was my mental health in the bin? I realise now that was a conscious decision, they knew but they didn't really want to *know*. One thing I did pointedly ask, what was the organisation going to do about this leak? Was there going to be any attempt to look into it? At that point I was still an employee, so where was that duty of care to me?

Nothing.

What did I expect?

So that was it.

Apart from one quick visit back in the office to say, "*Bye I'm done,*" the best part of a decade was guillotined. I had no idea what I was going to do next. The contrast to that day and the day I'd jumped around on the driveway wasn't one I could have known or imagined.

Looking back at what happened to me, my story is just another example of the glass cliff theory.

The Glass Cliff Theory

The glass cliff theory describes a real-world phenomenon in which women and people of colour are more likely to be appointed to precarious leadership positions in poorly performing organisations. It also shows that (generally) White men are more likely to be appointed to stable leadership positions in successful organisations

---

Why this metaphor of the glass cliff?

Because, having broken through the glass ceiling, we are left standing on the edge of a "glass cliff" with no support. The situation of being given that opportunity, that precarious, high-risk position which we then take on with vigor, without realising that we've effectively been walked to the edge of that glass cliff. We don't think about our own welfare, only the opportunity and what we need to do. It's high-risk, and high reward if we succeed. But what if we don't? We get put through the meat-grinder, which is exactly what happened to me. It was only through the love and support of my family that I didn't fall off that cliff, but I was hanging on by my fingertips at the end.

There are lots of people like me in organisations throughout the UK, and around the world, who are fighting because they believe, but don't realise the precarious position that they've been placed in. If in reading this you recognise yourself at all, I'd urge you to get a safety rope and a guide. Look after yourself first and foremost, because there are no guarantees that whichever system you are in will have anything but a performative interest in your wellbeing.

Learn the lessons from someone who put his own welfare to the back of the queue, until it was almost too late.

Don't be an idiot like me. Our families deserve more.

I had no idea what the future held for me, and I was anxious, but I knew I also needed to heal from what I had experienced in my time at the IOPC,

To give some sense of how I was feeling by that weekend, the clue was in the picture in my WhatsApp status. It was from the Shawshank Redemption, the moment where Andy Dufrensne looks up at the night sky which is pouring rain down on him. His arms are up, his eyes are closed and he's smiling. He has just escaped the Shawshank State Prison by crawling through a 500-yard sewage pipe full of shit.

He's come out the other side.

Now, he's free.

And so was I.

Chapter 12

When the end is not the ending

"Impossible is just a big word thrown around by small men who find it easier to live in the world they've been given than to explore the power they have to change it. Impossible is not a fact. It's an opinion. Impossible is not a declaration. It's a dare. Impossible is potential. Impossible is temporary. Impossible is nothing."

Muhammad Ali

I am looking at the water and it looks like glass.

It laps against my feet on the impossibly white sand of the beach. My bones creaking, I take a seat on the sand as I'm about to tick something off my bucket list. I get comfy and sit and watch over the next hour as the sun sets on the

349

horizon over the Caribbean Sea, while trying to ignore my OCD screaming against the sand wedged between my toes.

The scene begs a billion photos on my phone, so of course I oblige. The sky has all sorts of beautiful swirls of different hues of red, indigo, orange, and blue, dappling underneath the canopy of creamy clouds. It's the most breathtaking scene.

I take it all in, reflecting, enjoying the quiet in my mind and savouring the moment.

I whisper *Alhamdulillah* and for some reason, I remember my dad, and smile.

One year ago, almost to the day, I had walked away from a position that I had loved, but in a system that nearly broke me. I left with no job, not knowing what the future held for me.

One year on, I am sat on a beach halfway across the world in the Cayman Islands, not on a holiday but as guest of the Foreign Commonwealth Development Office, to speak to a policing audience as an expert in policing and inclusive cultures.

It's been over a year since I left the IOPC, and there's been a lot of time to reflect. In writing this book it has helped me to reflect and build my own understanding of the unique experiences I had at a historic time for policing in England & Wales. Truthfully, this book and my thoughts have evolved in my writing and reflections and so I'll try and share these briefly.

I've had many realisations as I've unpacked my experiences, one of which being that I was the unseen continuity in the system dealing with the worst cases concerning police misconduct in the recent history of the Metropolitan Police Service. All of those scandals, all of those headlines, I was always involved somewhere. To have been that connective thread was quite the epiphany and brings with it a level of experience and understanding that I probably have only scratched the surface of with this book.

I needed to step away from the IOPC to understand my own worth, I had become inculpated in a toxic culture. Breaking free from its grip had been incredibly difficult, but also one of the best decisions I've ever made. I hadn't realised it at the time, but nearly 40 years apart I had done what my dad had done all of those years ago and walked away from the security of a full-time job into the unknown. For very different reasons, but both of our decisions were based on our values.

That connection and coincidence made me smile, the fact that there was still a lot of my dad in me.

Since leaving the IOPC, a lot has happened. I got a senior role in a local authority, became a Trustee, have given guest lectures on the police accountability system in the UK, became a Fellow, delivered inputs to national and international policing, took on an ambassador role for a fantastic organisation focused on young people and I was even blessed enough to win a couple of major awards.

I have also had the chance to keep using my voice to speak about the issues in the media which are important to me on policing. I've contributed to a couple of significant pieces with the BBC focused on culture.

I've realised that what I was diminished for previously, were actually my strengths, and that my voice now carries resonance and authority when I speak about certain issues. This is something I'm currently just working through to understand where I can keep bringing light to the issues with the gift and freedom now of my own voice.

At the start of this book, I spoke about systems of denial and resisting them. I've tried to show through my story how multiple these can be and how they can deny your reality, and the resilience, stamina, and strength it takes to resist their multitude of gaslighting effects. From the societal racism and violence I experienced in my childhood, to the more subtle racial bias and marginalisation in the workplace, to the ultimate metaphor of denial that is the Metropolitan Police Service.

If you were to ask me about what I thought about the Met, I would tell you that as an organisation it is incapable of reform.

In my lectures I speak about how history has shown this to be true, time and time again. There is no basis to believe that the Met will reform itself to the recommendations made in the Casey review. There is an engrained arrogance and denial stitched into the fabric of the leadership of New Scotland Yard, whoever the incumbents are at that time. I believe the only option is for fundamental structural reform of the Met, as happened in Northern Ireland with the former Royal Ulster Constabulary. This was reformed to the new Police Service Northern Ireland with a new structure and focus on learning from its predecessors' failings. I see no way round this.

I also then come to the bitter and unexpected realisation that my own organisation was also one of these very systems of denial.

It was part of the problem but never realised it, and therefore for all of those years, despite my best intentions, so was I. The IOPC and the whole police misconduct system in England and Wales needs an end-to-end review and overhaul. The recent tinkering proposed to the IOPC[45], and the disciplinary system is just nibbling at the edges. Families and police officers need a system that's fit for the legitimately different societal expectations we have of policing now, and that reflects the demands and huge pressures of modern policing in a fairer way. This work needs and deserves a Royal Commission.

As for the here and now, the IOPC requires brave leadership to call things out when they

---

[45] Independent Office for Police Conduct: Public body review 2024 - GOV.UK (www.gov.uk)

need to be called out, and to go where the evidence takes it. Its DNA is from the Stephen Lawrence Inquiry, a fact that merits cognisance more than just the singular performative posting on Stephen Lawrence Day, but also on the other 364 days a year. I remain pessimistic that the courage to stick its head above the parapet exists at the most senior levels within the organisation.

I also reflect on the reality of what happened when someone like me came into the system, and tried with all of their ability to drive change in the limited way that they could. The system's response was much like the response of an immune system fighting an infection. I was seeking to address elephants in the room and make change in the system. The depressing reality for me, was that even at the age I am, and with the seniority I had, the spectre of racism was still there impeding me.

I will say this now, I am nothing special.

Bang average.

And yet, it took someone like me to come in and lead in the way that I did to engender the small measure of change in the system I managed while I held my post. I don't celebrate that fact. I take sadness from it because it shouldn't have taken that, and what does that say about what and who went before me?

The only reason any of this was possible, that I did what I did, was because of those precious values I hold so dear and how I always align myself to them. Leading and living like this has enabled me to travel through the difficult terrain that I have in my life and career, always pointing me to my true north. Always, keeping me constant in my direction, in my aspiration, in how I carry myself.

I then imagine what if others around me in the system I operated in, followed that path in the same way? Imagine the change we could achieve together?

Because *nothing* will change until *we* change and learn to lead in a different way. If I could bring the level of disruption I did to the system, then what could a united movement do? If we all pointed in the same direction, working to improve the issues of culture within policing and provide the necessary courage within the police accountability system?

Until we get the leadership we deserve in these positions, we will remain in a cyclical holding pattern of the issues I've described in this book, round and round, again and again.

Making change isn't easy, but if someone like me was able to do what I've done in my life, then why can't you?

Everyone has that capacity inside them, but it takes courage to unlock this within ourselves, courage which can be cultivated with the small incremental steps that no one else needs to see until it becomes second nature, muscle memory.

Honestly, just try it.

The sun has now set.

I take the straight walk back to my hotel, which is only ten or so minutes in the distance. The night sky is lit with thousands of stars that are free from the smog of any light pollution. I can't help but look up and marvel.

Tomorrow I will be speaking about my personal experience and learning on male allyship, to nearly 100 of the officers in the Royal Cayman

Islands Police Service. I know what I'm going to say but I'd like to run through it one more time to make sure I provide the best input possible. I feel that responsibility.

My journey has taken me halfway across the world to this beautiful point. But here's the thing. I don't think I'm finished yet.

I feel a restlessness in my soul and know that there is something more, something else for me to give in public service. I'm not sure what that is yet, but it's a feeling I have in the pit of my stomach that won't go.

The feeling speaks to one of my favourite quotes from Kurt Hahn:

"There is more to us than we know. If we can be made to see it, perhaps for the rest of our lives we will be unwilling to settle for less."

So, I'll keep following my true north and see where that takes me.

It's got me this far.

Reviews for True North

Professor Jonathan Crego

"I have now read your entire book. I have cried whilst reading, taking time to ponder on its deep meaning. It is a profound outpouring, brave, honest and real. You articulate your personal struggles and triumphs and whilst they are upsetting and difficult to read, your love of your family and colleagues and faith and their love for you, shines through. It is a story that needs to be told."

Professor Sarah Charman

In his desire to both challenge and change cultures of prejudice and discrimination within policing, Sal has written a brutally honest and highly readable account of the professional and personal impact of 'poking the bear'. Starting with his first memories of racist abuse on the streets of Kilmarnock in the 1970s, Sal's journey takes him to be the most senior person of colour at the Independent Office for Police Conduct as Regional Director for London. There he makes the monumental decision to, for the first time, expose the realities of what toxic cultures in policing actually look like and in doing so, fundamentally challenges the prevailing status quo. This highly personal account of 'faith, family and fight' invites us to reflect on our assumptions, our biases and importantly, our leadership. Never has there been a better time to adopt Sal's invitation to 'rise by lifting each other' and to acknowledge that 'nothing will change until we change'.

Dr Michael Shiner

Part memoire, part autobiography, True North is a tour de force that tells the story of how a 'shy, wee boy' with a stutter made his way to the top of the police complaints system and of what happened when he got there. It is a deeply personal and inspiring story of survival, resilience, and resourcefulness, of finding and holding on to your true self. But there is another parallel story of power, politics and (not) belonging. As the outsider's outsider, Sal Naseem takes us into the remote corners of the regulatory state, shining a light into the shadows to reveal a bewildering world of smoke and mirrors. The result is not easy to read, but it is vitally important. There are highs and lows, there is some humour amongst the tragedy, but mostly there is disappointment. Disappointment over the failure of the police complaints system to deliver on its mission and the "witch hunt" that left the author with little option but to resign. Part of the tragedy here is that Sal was exactly where he was supposed to be, doing exactly what he was supposed to be doing. He was qualified for the role, committed to the mandate, and took pride in a job well done. His mistake - if we can call it that - was to expect the system to fulfil its stated purpose: to follow the evidence and conduct investigations without fear or favour. The final irony is that the system needs more Sals if it is to properly fulfil its stated mission and needs to take account of what they have to say. True North is a must read for anyone interested in policing, racism, regulation and organisational leadership.

Sue Fish OBE

Like everything else Sal Naseem has done True North is courageous and a values driven read. Sal hasn't shirked from describing the harsh realities and consequences of racism, loss, and establishment denial. The cost of staying true to your True North hit me like a sledgehammer – and with rather a lot of personal resonance. Sal has laid bare the hypocrisy of institutions (the MPS in particular) who profess to value diversity, change and reform, but actually it's all performative bullshit. Institutions such as police forces – and in his case the MPS – are far too vested in the status quo and whatever change he brought much will have been reclaimed and the narrative changed to suit the institution – however in writing this book Sal has reminded me why he, me, and countless others are determined to follow our values and how much organisations and institutions need us more than we need them. Sal's writing also has his trademark empathy and humility throughout it, and not withstanding what society and our institutions put him through he has emerged with honour, integrity, perspective, and his values intact – from my experience that is a rare commodity and truly inspiring. I am really looking forward to his next chapter.

About the Author

Sal Naseem is the former Regional Director for London at the Independent Office for Police Conduct, where he spent the best part of a decade working in the police accountability framework in England and Wales. Sal is currently Assistant Director of Insight, Policy & Strategy, a Senior Associate Fellow at The Police Foundation and an independent panel member at the National Fire Chiefs Council, supporting their work on culture and inclusion and a Trustee at the Centre for Justice Innovation.

Sal has been listed as one of the top 10 voices in the world on anti-discrimination on LinkedIn by Favikon in 2024. Honoured as one of the 50 most influential people driving change in the UK through inclusion in the Diversity Power List 2023/2024, and also recognised as one of the most inspirational leaders on inclusion by D&I Leaders 2024.

Sal has worked on some of the most high-profile misconduct cases featuring the Metropolitan Police Service in recent years.

As the Strategic Lead on Discrimination his work focused on stop & search, racism, misogyny, and police culture. Sal sat on the NPCC Police Race Action Plan Board, and the NPCC National DEI Board as an independent member.

Sal is also a media commentator and uses his platform to talk about male allyship as a necessity in the fight against male violence against women and girls, and broader issues related to inclusion.

Sal holds a law degree from the University of Glasgow and is a Fellow of the Royal Society of Arts and Society of Leadership Fellows.

Printed in Great Britain
by Amazon

52796518R00205